Title: Centering Multilingual Learners
Subtitle: An Essential How-To Guide for Secondary Teachers
ISBN: 978-1-965016-35-0

Cover and illustrations by Laura Serra *lauraserra.org*
Design by Matthew Coles and Stephen Coles
Set in Infini by Sandrine Nugue

Feedback, questions, and your stories from the classroom are welcome!
marileecolesritchie.com

INTRODUCTION

This guide book will provide you, secondary teachers, with essential tools to support Multilingual Learners (MLs) in your classes. My hope is that after reading this book, you'll have two main takeaways. One, you'll realize that your classroom is enhanced when you are fortunate enough to have Multilingual Learners in it. Two, you'll have the tools to support MLs in your classroom and see their growth without compromising the learning of primarily English speakers.

I dedicate this book to all the teachers who creatively design curricula to meet the needs of Multilingual Learners and learn from them.

Book Organization

I developed a graph that encompasses the essential components ("the Five Cs") for teachers of MLs. They are:

- Critically Conscious Classroom
- Connection with Community
- Context for Content
- Collaboration for Content
- Choice in Assessment

I explain each of these components in separate chapters along with practical tips, graphs, and examples to help you implement them in your classroom. At the end of the book, you'll find an easy-to-use glossary of key terms.

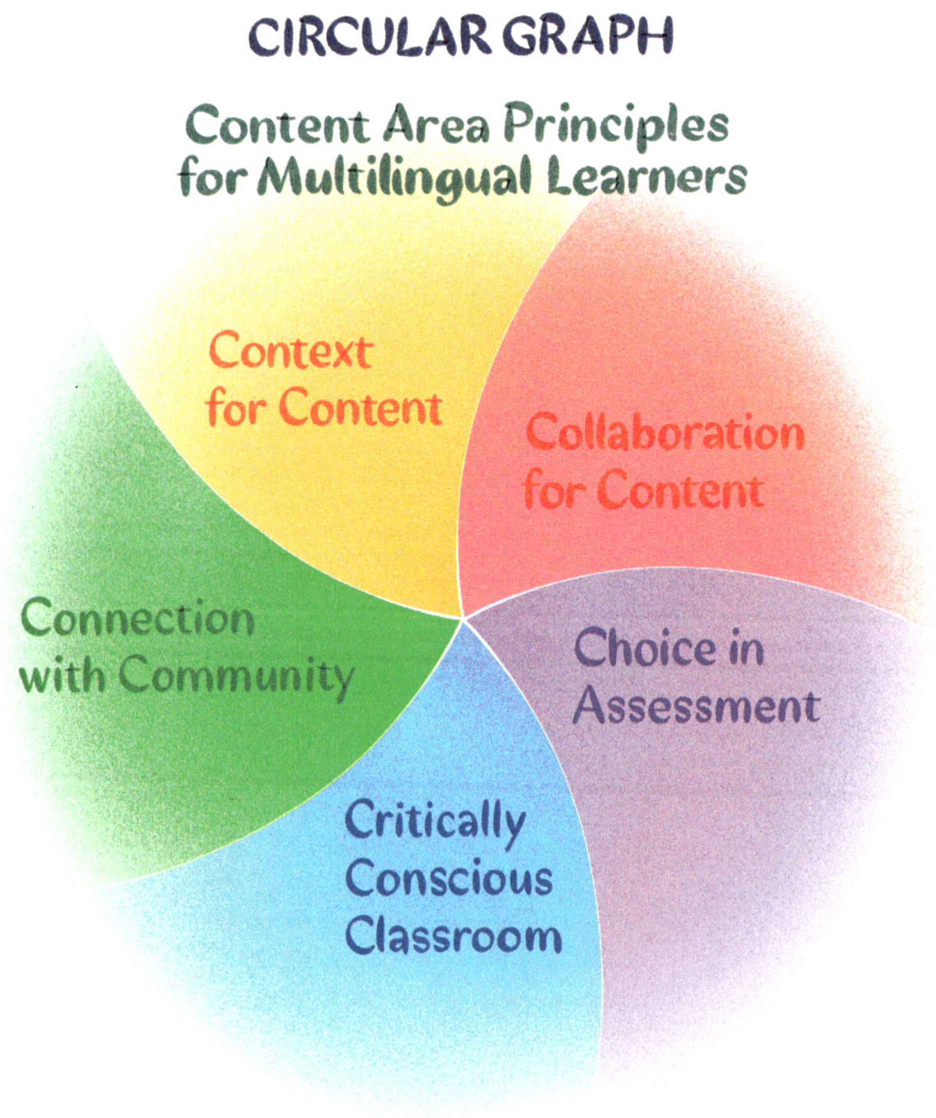

CIRCULAR GRAPH

Content Area Principles
for Multilingual Learners

Context
for Content

Collaboration
for Content

Connection
with Community

Choice in
Assessment

Critically
Conscious
Classroom

I have organized the book into seven chapters.

The introduction will lay the groundwork of my philosophy of teaching Multilingual Learners (MLs) in the secondary context, and will explain the foundations of my philosophy of teaching.

Chapter One describes how to physically create a *critically conscious classroom* (CCC). I describe how to set up your classroom and how to consider all the senses the students experience when they walk in. What do they see, hear, smell, and feel when they walk in that lets them know they belong?

Chapter Two explores ways to connect with community by what you do inside and outside the classroom.

Chapter Three focuses on the importance of context in language learning. Students need to be able to see what they are learning. Dr. James Cummins, an often-cited bilingual educator and researcher, created a graph as a guideline for teachers when planning curriculum. He introduced the concepts of BICS and CALP, which have been critiqued by some researchers but can be a helpful starting guide for content teachers as they begin to think about how they can make their lessons more contextual.

Chapter Four delves into how organizing context can increase content comprehension. This chapter provides descriptions of special tools for you and examples of tasks for your students that will connect them to the content.

Chapter Five demonstrates how important collaboration is for truly understanding course content. This chapter suggests lots of ways to encourage collaboration in meaningful ways and specific elements you want to consider for MLs.

Chapter Six focuses on a critical element in teaching assessment. In this chapter, I advocate for the importance of choice in assessment. I include lots of ways to find out what your students know at their language level so they stretch but are not overwhelmed.

I conclude in Chapter Seven with a few tips for supporting students who have experienced trauma, and ideas for avoiding tokenism. These two issues often arise when teaching MLs and are not often addressed in books about language acquisition.

I wrote this book for teachers I know who have intellectual agility, compassionate hearts, and creative minds. They want to support their students but would appreciate a guide to connect them to specific strategies. This is an essential guide—it is compact, researched-based, and includes the most basic supports. I wanted to make it accessible with ideas that can be implemented in the educational structure.

A biology teacher recently called me and asked how they could support a student from Guatemala with only a beginning level of English. The student was informally educated about the world, having traveled across Mexico via train and foot and having worked on the family farm, but had little formal schooling due to their economic condition. Despite the challenge, this student has the potential to enhance the biology classroom, if the teacher can implement the Five Cs I describe here. This is just one of many conversations I've had with former students.

I'm impressed that you, the reader, are here. I believe you picked up this book because you want to be the most effective teacher possible for the MLs in your classes. I use an ecological approach for supporting MLs through the following steps*:

- Sustain academic rigor
- Hold high expectations
- Encourage metacognitive processes about learning
- Engage in quality teacher and student-to-student interactions
- Sustain a language focus while supporting all languages in their repertoires
- Develop a culturally sustaining curriculum to meet students' lived experiences

** Adapted from WestED's Quality Teaching for English Learners*[1]

Through building curriculum and pedagogy on these principles, I have seen MLs, English-dominant students, and teachers thrive.

Norming the Term "Multilingualism"

Using the term "Multilingual Learner" rather than "English Learner" is intentional. "English Learner" ignores the fact that a student is adding a language to at least one they already know. I've been inspired by the work of Dover and Rodriquez-Valls[2], who developed and collected data on an after-school program called "Language Explorers" in a public school district. This program is aligned with the notion that multilingual classrooms should be the norm. They explain that in an English-only classroom, multilingual students are forced into daily confrontations with explicit and implicit actions that position monolingualism as the norm[3]. You might be thinking, "But English is the norm and they have to learn it to be able to take tests, write essays, and more importantly, find a job." Hear me out. When teachers embrace and highlight all of MLs' identities, including cultural and linguistic, their language abilities grow and their understanding of the content expands.

Because it is not the norm, I am asking you to be courageous in your desire to create these multilingual and culturally expanding oases. With time, they might not be oases because your entire school and then districts will provide fertile ground for MLs. Your students, whether

---

1 www.qtel.wested.org

2 Dover, Alison G., and Fernando Ferran Rodríguez-Valls. *Radically inclusive teaching with newcomer and emergent plurilingual students: Braving up.* Teachers College Press, 2022.

3 Flores, Nelson, and Jonathan Rosa. "Undoing appropriateness: Raciolinguistic ideologies and language diversity in education." *Harvard Educational Review* 85.2 (2015): 149-171.

classified as English Learners or monolingual, will stretch their cognitive, emotional, and linguistic abilities by experimenting with language in creative and intellectually deep ways.

I align with the work of Paris and Alim[4], who describe the most welcoming spaces for all students as "culturally sustaining." In these spaces, teachers and administrators like you put front and center the lived experiences of students who have previously been regulated to the margins.

Factor	Culturally Sustaining Approach	Asset-based Approach	Deficit-based Approach
Primary language	• Work on using it in the classroom often • Implement full immersion program	• Gift to be recognized • Helpful for future employment	• Problem to overcome • Barrier to learning
Families and Community of MLs	• Enhance the learning and development of all students • Invite them to present in the classroom and school	• Engaged in their child(ren)'s education • Encourage interaction at home with all their linguistic backgrounds • Acknowledge their culture and lived experiences as a benefit to student learning	• Discourage cultural learning and practices at home • Make derogatory comments about MLs' lived experiences
Neighborhood	• Develop critical community engagement with businesses and other organizations in neighborhoods where MLs live	• Ask neighborhood businesses to contribute finances or products to the school	• Call the neighborhood a "ghetto" • Describe the neighborhood as "sketchy" or "dangerous" • Make comments such as, "Have you seen where they live?"
MLs' Countries of Origins	• Study the resources and positive practices of the country	• Acknowledge the countries • Pin the locations of the countries on a map	• Discuss the country with a pity narrative • Only focus on the war or economic insecurity of the country

You disrupt the idea that English is the only language welcome in the school and expand the notion that all grow and learn when multiple languages are spoken and written. Use their cultural knowledge, lived experiences, concerns, and frames of reference to every lesson you plan.

Culturally Sustaining, Asset-based, and Deficit-based Approaches

Do these categories resonate with you? What do you need to shift in thoughts and actions to better sustain the cultures of your MLs?

---

4 Paris, Django, and H. Samy Alim, eds. *Culturally sustaining pedagogies. Teaching and learning for justice in a changing world.* Teachers College Press, 2017.

Language is Dynamic

Many researchers postulate that language is dynamic—ever changing—and that there isn't a "right" way of communicating. Language cannot be isolated and cut off from context[5]. The idea of "pure" or "high" language is socially constructed and divorced from everyday language use. Of course, some standards are more acceptable in different settings, but even those can be challenged. Think about the word "sick," which used to only mean "a person who isn't well." Today, *sick* can mean "amazing" or "cool," but cool used to mean "an almost cold temperature." And so on.

I believe in the importance of teaching language as dynamic to our students and accepting that stance as students interact and produce material. You can still require that some assignments meet the standard English requirements and teach them that this standard is accepted through linguistic power (or Standardized English). In addition, I would challenge you to accept some assignments in the MLs' community languages and explain to the entire class why that's important.

It's fascinating to learn that in the last hundred years, cores of articles based on linguistic research demonstrate that affirming a student's linguistic heritage is paramount for them to acquire a new language.[6][7][8][9][10] Still, much of state and federal legislation focuses on an "English only" type of curriculum. Many educational agencies use deficit language such as *Limited English Proficient, English Language Learner*, or *ESL Student*. In reality, every ML comes to class with a rich repertoire of language that they can use to communicate and learn if they are supported. I used the term *Multilingual Learner* because it is more accurate and encompasses the assets that a student brings to the learning context.

Language is Culture

Language is intrinsically connected to culture[11][12];among others). It is how we communicate with each other, build relationships, and create community. Communication through language is a component of any society. Throughout time, as languages began to develop, cultural communities

5 García, Ofelia, and Rosario Torres-Guevara. "11 Monoglossic Ideologies and Language Policies in the Education of US Latinas/os." *Handbook of Latinos and education: Theory, research, and practice* (2009): 182.

6 Cummins, Jim. "Cognitive/Academic Language Proficiency, Linguistic Interdependence, the Optimum Age Question and Some Other Matters. Working Papers on Bilingualism, No. 19." (1979).

7 Krashen, Stephen D. "The input hypothesis: Issues and implications." (1985).

8 Tarone, Elaine, and Merrill Swain. "A sociolinguistic perspective on second language use in immersion classrooms." *The Modern Language Journal* 79.2 (1995): 166–178.

9 Valdés, Guadalupe. "Latin@ s and the intergenerational continuity of Spanish: The challenges of curricularizing language." *International Multilingual Research Journal* 9.4 (2015): 253–273.

10 Wright, Wayne E. "The political spectacle of Arizona's Proposition 203." *Educational Policy* 19.5 (2005): 662–700.

11 Oxford, Rebecca L., and Christina Gkonou. "Interwoven: Culture, language, and learning strategies." Studies in Second Language Learning and Teaching 8.2 (2018): 403–426.

12 Paris, Django, and H. Samy Alim, eds. *Culturally sustaining pedagogies: Teaching and learning for justice in a changing world.* Teachers College Press, 2017

developed collective understandings through sounds. Over time, these sounds and their implied meanings became commonplace, and language was formed. Intercultural communication is a symbolic process whereby social reality is constructed, maintained, repaired, and transformed.

Why are these ideas about language foundational for teachers of middle and high school students? For me, understanding the connection of language to culture helps me see how central language is to identity. My respect for students' languages that might be different from mine increases and encourages connection with my students. With this understanding, the idea of shutting down MLs' primary language use seems absurd. I want to include their languages and allow MLs to draw upon them, and also try to learn some of their language as a way to connect.

I read a beautiful example of embracing languages in an article by Ofelia Garcia, Kate Seltzer, and Daria Witt[13]. These researchers describe how a high school English teacher disrupts linguistic inequities by holding the paradox of supporting development of MLs' language practice in English and at the same time valuing the interrelationship with their primary-language practices. This high school teacher values collaboration, language, content integration, and a strong connection between language and culture[14]. Because she doesn't speak all fifteen languages within her high school classroom, the teacher relies on her MLs to bridge the gap and strongly encourages them to share their communities' funds of knowledge . She takes the understanding they share and connects it to the core goals she is required to teach. Of course, this takes more work that just teaching the same content year after year, but the excitement of connection and co-learning with the students makes up for this. For specific examples, I'll be sharing a "translanguaging" section.

Stage	Description
Stage 1: Pre-Production	During this stage, the student is primarily silent. They observe and listen to new words and gain an understanding of the language as their brain collects data.
Stage 2: Early Production	At this stage, the student starts to practice pronouncing new words, and typically learns at least one thousand new words and their meanings. They also start using their new words to speak in short phrases.
Stage 3: Speech Emergence	Vocabulary continues to expand, and a student will know a minimum of three thousand words by the end of this stage. They start to speak in longer phrases and sentences and begin to ask questions. In addition, at this stage they will start reading and writing assignments.
Stage 4: Intermediate Fluency	Students start to think and form responses in the new language. By the end of this stage, most learners will have a vocabulary of about six thousand words and their meanings. They are also speaking more fluently and continuing to improve upon their reading and writing abilities.
Stage 5: Advanced Fluency	Students who reach this stage continue to improve upon and expand their vocabulary and abilities in their second language, but can engage in mainstream classes without a lot of scaffolding.

13 García, Ofelia, Kate Seltzer, and Daria Witt. "Disrupting linguistic inequalities in US urban classrooms: The role of translanguaging." *The Multilingual Edge of Education* (2018): 41–66.

14 González, Norma, Luis C. Moll, and Cathy Amanti, eds. *Funds of knowledge: Theorizing practices in households, communities, and classrooms.* Routledge, 2006.

Five Stages of Language Acquisition

A key challenge in designing lessons for MLs is knowing what to expect. Most students will go through five stages of language learning. The amount of time spent in each stage depends upon several factors, like a learner's age, background knowledge in the subject matter, cognitive abilities, desire to take risks, affective filter, their commitment, and support of the program and classrooms. These stages could be identified by their intake information, but not necessarily. Sometimes, instead of assigning MLs a stage of language acquisition after placement testing, they will be assigned a WIDA number.

WIDA Can-Do Descriptors

WIDA (World-Class Instructional Design and Assessment) is a research and professional development organization that believes that every child brings valuable resources to the education space. They explain: "Children and youth who are linguistically and culturally diverse bring a unique set of assets that have the potential to enrich the experiences of all learners and educators. Educators can draw on these assets for the benefit of both the learners themselves and for everyone in the community."

By focusing on what language learners can do, teachers and administrators send a powerful message that children and youth from diverse linguistic and cultural backgrounds contribute to the vibrancy of K–12 schools. The *Can-Do Descriptors* have been created by teachers, primarily for teachers who work with Multilingual Learners. These descriptors for the four language domains—listening, speaking, reading, and writing—and six levels of English-language proficiency are based on the WIDA English Language Proficiency Standards.

The following WIDA charts available online are helpful guides when planning curriculum:

- WIDA Can-do Descriptors for Grades 6–8
  wida.wisc.edu/sites/default/files/resource/CanDo-KeyUses-Gr-6-8.pdf
- WIDA Can-do Descriptors for Grades 9–12
  wida.wisc.edu/sites/default/files/resource/CanDo-KeyUses-Gr-9-12.pdf

In summary, a research review conducted by Faltis et al. (2010)[15] suggests the following competencies for secondary teachers of Multilingual Learners (MLs):

- Understand second-language acquisition as participation and identity.
- Plan for and use theme-based content where concepts, genres, and specialized vocabulary are spiraled and used in multiple ways.
- Build on students' background knowledge and experiences.
- Know and advocate for legal rights of Multilingual Learners.
- Scaffold instruction for variation in schooling experiences of MLs.
- Integrate MLs with dominante English speakers so they can all learn from one another.

All of these competencies are included in the 5Cs I've outlined in this book.

15 Faltis, Christian, M. Beatriz Arias, and Frank Ramírez-Marín. "Identifying relevant competencies for secondary teachers of English learners." *Bilingual Research Journal* 33.3 (2010): 307–328.

CHAPTER ONE

1

A Critically Conscious Classroom

"The teacher is of course an artist, but being an artist does not mean that he or she can make the profile, can shape the students. What the educator does in teaching is to make it possible for the students to become themselves."

— PAOLO FREIRE

I'm not one who normally pays attention to decor in classrooms—creating bulletin boards was one of my most anxiety-producing thoughts when I was a classroom teacher. I've since changed my mind on what needs to be on the wall, especially when it comes to Multilingual Learners who often don't see themselves at school. Just recently, I walked into a high school English classroom. I immediately felt calm and motivated. The student's personal artwork adorned the walls alongside poetry by Langston Hughes, while string lights illuminated a free tea station. A welcoming sign featuring "hello" in various languages greeted visitors near the entrance. Motivational posters authored by renowned BIPOC figures adorned the walls, and desks were arranged in tables with tennis balls affixed to chair legs to minimize noise during group activities.

You might feel similarly. With all that is required of you in secondary life, the task of decorating your classroom might come last. I certainly understand that. This chapter is to help you create that welcoming class for all, without spending a lot of time or money.

How you use your classroom space can significantly support how MLs learn to use their learning environment, it can also be triggering by signally that people who look like them don't belong there. The classroom space is considered a "third teacher" within the Reggio Emilia approach. Using the classroom space to signal welcome, inspire curiosity, enable discovery learning is the first step is supporting learning.

In 2015, Barrett et al. studied 153 K–12 classrooms[1]. They concluded that students gained the most from classes when the walls contained significant information. They advise the material put on the walls be stimulating and student creative, but not messy. They stated that wall displays should be created to give the classroom a lively atmosphere, without being chaotic. To maintain an optimal balance, they suggest that between 20–50 percent of the wall space be left unoccupied.

Drawing on research, conversations with MLs, and practicing teachers, I have created a list that can help you get started in meeting that goal.

Wall Space

At the beginning of the school year, you may want to establish designated areas for dedicated to classroom goals. But a lot of the wall space should be open based on what your students decide. It's an empowering idea to discuss the purpose what is placed on the wall with your students. When students are invited to engage in the purpose of what is there and why—the investment in it is far greater. They will most likely pay closer attention to it. This is a great opportunity to share basics about becoming a community of learners and some of the principles of language acquisition. When this is established, all students, those who are dominate English speakers and those that speak other languages, will have a better understanding of what is on the walls and why. They will more likely look to the items on the wall for ideas and inspiration, reference material, reflection, or for looking at other's thinking. Purposeful postings can enhance independent learning[2].

---

1 Barrett, Peter, Fay Davies, Yufan Zhang, and Lucinda Barrett. "The impact of classroom design on pupils' learning: Final results of a holistic, multi-level analysis." *Building and Environment* 89 (2015): 118–133.

2 Ferlazzo, Larry, and Katie Hull Sypnieski. *The ELL Teacher's Toolbox: Hundreds of Practical Ideas to Support Your Students*. John Wiley & Sons, 2018.

LABELING IN DIFFERENT LANGUAGES

Center a variety of languages by posting them visibly all around your classroom.

This might not be the first thing that comes to mind in secondary schools and you may feel it to be juvenile, but teachers tell me that all students find it interesting to see different languages posted. These labels don't have to be professionally made. I would suggest getting the students in your class involved. At the beginning of the year, have them look around the room and decide what the most important items and structures are to understand concepts for the class. Once you have that information, you can recruit primary speakers of the different languages to help you create the labels.

Center a variety of languages by posting them visibly all around your classroom.

HANG A MAP

Make sure a world map is visible with push pins indicating students' countries of origin. Get a simple inexpensive map and hang it on a bulletin board where you can insert pins. I would suggest the maps that (insert US less primary ones) and that include indigenous tribal lands (you could also insert those after). Encourage students to put pins in the parts of the country and world where they were born or spent a large amount of time. Both students born outside of the United States and elsewhere should be included.

POSTERS WITH CONTENT

Motivational and content rich posters are quite common on many classroom walls. Hanging images of role models and their quote help MLs gain a greater sense of belonging and aspiration, especially when their backgrounds and interests are represented. Key goal is to strive for inclusion, but avoid token or stereotypical representations.

When creating or purchasing posters, consider choosing those from that depict people from different countries, disabilities, races, genders. It's especially important for them to see their cultures and races represented in the content areas you teach. For example, math teachers could find pictures of mathematicians from various racial and ethnic backgrounds. Science teachers can find scientists in action from all across the globe representing a variety of skin tone, genders, and locations.

Students can actively engage in creating these charts to deepen their understanding of content. Instead of buying posters, the content can be constructed by students with a focus on

learning by doing. The more you can involve students in decisions about what's posted and what each poster or student evidence says about the learning taking place.

Visual aids on the wall such as anchor charts, maps, and diagrams can be especially helpful for MLs especially when they are referenced. When these visuals reinforce a lesson, it can reinforce student learning through "optimiz[ing] decision-making" in chaotic, quickly changing environments[3]. The posters should be rotated to connect to the content focus[4].

STUDENT WORK

Students are drawn to work produced by themselves other students. Creating space for published work, or final products can be a motivating way to celebrate a product. Involving the students in this process adds to the reflective, metacognitive process. Barrett et al.[5] claim that students not only feel a greater sense of responsibility for their learning, but are also more likely to remember the content. When students decide what goes up on the wall and why, more voices and ideas are present when they know the work is going up. Students could choose a piece of their process work and ask for feedback or they could choose something that is finished or publishable.

---

3 Richards, Blake A., and Paul W. Frankland. "The persistence and transience of memory." *Neuron* 94.6 (2017): 1071–1084.

4 Bui, Dung C., and Mark A. McDaniel. "Enhancing learning during lecture note-taking using outlines and illustrative diagrams." *Journal of Applied Research in Memory and Cognition* 4.2 (2015): 129–135.

5 Barrett, Nathan, et al. "Working with what they have: Professional development as a reform strategy in rural schools." *Journal of Research in Rural Education* (Online) 30.10 (2015): 1.

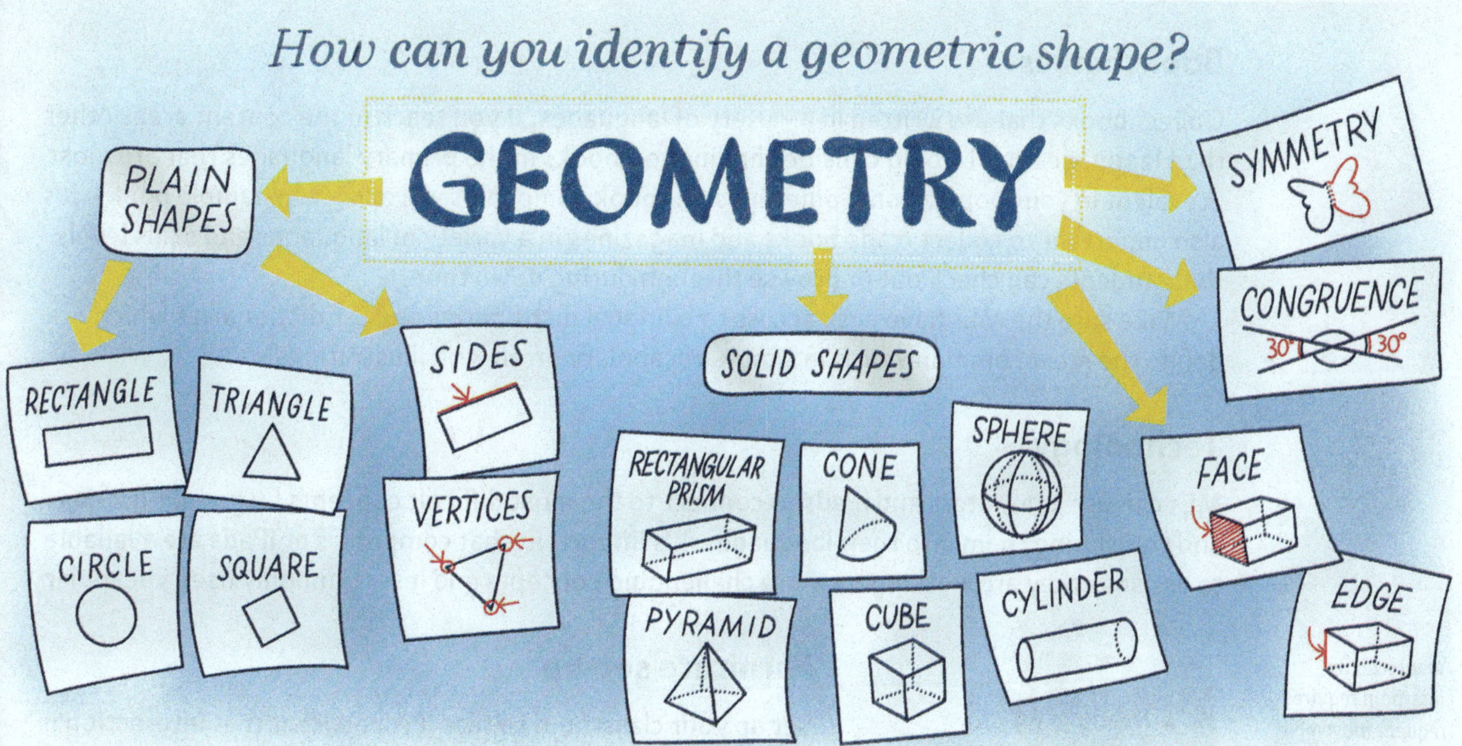

PHOTOS OF STUDENTS WORKING

Another engaging and motivating idea is to create an area of the classroom for photos of students working on hands-on projects. This can emphasize the idea of process, not just final product. Most students love to the see photos of themselves and their classmates at work. It's helpful to place not only pictures of students working but also the quotes, sketches, mindmaps that they have produced. Celebrating process-oriented work in process demonstrates that you value the process of learning.

COMMON PHRASES ANCHOR

Create a poster or handout for students stating the most common phrases with translations or graphics that are common in your classroom. Consider the content area language in addition to the structural language that is most common in the daily routine of your classroom. Class expectations are posted and translated in the students' languages.

AGENDA WITH OBJECTIVES/ESSENTIAL QUESTIONS

Routines are important for all students but they are especially helpful for MLs who may need to use context to understand key ideas. It's helpful if you have an agenda clearly written in the same place each day or that it is the first slide of your PowerPoint. In addition, adding language and content objectives or essential questions.

Bookshelves

Collect books that are written in a variety of languages. If you teach in the content areas other than language arts, I would consider finding textbooks in the primary languages that are most prevalent in your population. Sometimes textbook companies will give away sample books. It's also important to collect trade books and magazines in a variety of languages and skills levels that students can check out or browse through during down time.

Make sure the MLs have easy access to bilingual dictionaries and ESL dictionaries which define the most common words in simple vocabulary often with illustrations.

Technology

MLs can use computers and iPads to connect to the most difficult concepts by googling ideas and translating them into their languages. It's important that computers or iPads are available to assist as they are working on more challenging concepts and less commonly used vocabulary.

An interactive classroom requires frequent movement. Prepare tables and chairs with soft feet to allow them to move quietly.

Furniture set-up

Set up your classroom so that it is apparent that interaction is central to what you do there. Move desks into clusters or ask for tables where students sit groups. If you don't have chairs that can be moved easily without noises, consider getting used tennis balls to put on the bottom of the legs so that they can glide to different groups without distraction.

Music

Play music from a variety of cultures and languages when the students walk into class and when they are working on different tasks. You can have the students take turns sharing their music and the meanings behind the lyrics.

Natural Light

Natural light can create an atmosphere of learning. No, really? Students who experience more natural light in their classroom can improve learning in math and reading[6]. If you don't have natural light through windows, it's important that the room is well lit[7].

Enter your classroom with new eyes. Even better, ask a few seasoned MLs to help evaluate your space. Here's a classroom inventory you can use to evaluate what is working and what you could add to create a more inclusive and motivating learning space.

---

6 Cheryan, Sapna, et al. "Designing classrooms to maximize student achievement." *Policy Insights from the Behavioral and Brain Sciences* 1.1 (2014): 4–12.

7 Barrett, Nathan, et al. "Working with what they have: Professional development as a reform strategy in rural schools." *Journal of Research in Rural Education* (Online) 30.10 (2015): 1.

CLASSROOM INVENTORY

- *Labeling in multiple languages*
- *Map with pushpins representing where students have lived*
- *Content rich posters with multiple representations*
- *Student work*
- *Photos of students engaging in projects*
- *Bookshelves with books in multiple languages and dictionaries*
- *Technology for translations*
- *Furniture set up for interaction*
- *Play music from a variety of cultures and languages*
- *Natural light*

CHAPTER TWO

Connection with Community

2

"As a classroom community, our capacity to generate excitement is deeply affected by our interest in one another, in hearing one another's voices, in recognizing one another's presence.[1]"

— BELL HOOKS

1 bell hooks, *Teaching to Transgress: Education as the Practice of Freedom* (Oxfordshire, England: Routledge, 1994).

This quote by one of my intellectual and scholarly mentors, bell hooks, has guided me as I develop community in my classes. Some of my most poignant memories of teaching happened outside the classroom, when I made home visits, attended a *quinceañera*, purchased food from a local market owned by a student's parent, and took MLs to compete in the Future Business Leaders of America.

Higher engagement and achievement is more prevalent when students see their home language, culture, and identities authentically appreciated in the classroom and community. Building relationships with students, students one to each other, and students with the larger community is imperative to building up the knowledge of students' individual and collective experiences. I can recall countless stories of when getting to know a student made a profound difference in my life and theirs. Of course, this is key for all students, but it is imperative with MLs as their experience in the community is new and extra challenging in the process of learning a new language.

How do you set up a classroom where students feel comfortable sharing their stories? How do you model genuine dialogue? It might be helpful if we model this kind of interchange for our students. For MLs, in particular, their stories might not be typical of a student who grew up monolingually and White in the United States. They might not feel comfortable sharing unless they observe meaningful interchanges between you and other students—and it's even better when they see it student to student.

A powerful way to develop rapport that leads to meaningful relationship happens right before class starts. Examples include teachers meeting their students at the door each day to greet them by name. Another way is to show a visual chart indicating if they would like a fist bump, handshake, or high five.

Each school and district have policies and protocols for entering students. I have found that many teachers are not aware of their ability to ask for that data for use in planning and connection. Ask your instructional leaders what intake data are available to build a background for your MLs.

IDEAS FOR DEVELOPING RELATIONSHIPS

Expanded Home Language Survey: Linguistic Assets for Your Content Areas

Every new public-school student must complete a Home Language Survey. According to the United States Department of Education[2]:

> Local Education Agencies must identify in a timely manner EL [or Multilingual] students in need of language assistance services. The home language survey (HLS) is a questionnaire given to parents or guardians that helps schools and LEAs identify which students are potential ELs and who will require assessment of their English language proficiency (ELP) to determine whether they are eligible for language assistance services. Many SEAs either require a state-developed HLS or provide a sample for LEAs to use; thus, it is advisable to check with the SEA about HLS guidance.

The information on the form is a small snapshot into their language life. I suggest creating an additional survey for your understanding as a classroom teacher, because the survey doesn't delve into the nuances of language use in different settings and with their family and friend relationships. Garcia and Torres-Guevara[3] explain the importance of moving away from viewing languages as static, dichotomous, and discrete and moving toward dynamic and contextually situated. Why is this important for you to know? Understanding that language is situational allows you to plan with more openness. You can relax, knowing that your students will draw on their linguistic repertoire without worrying about pushing them to only stick with English.

MLs arrive with varying levels of background in English language development and bring a rich variety of multiple language assets that can add knowledge to your classroom. When you understand that language background better, you can identify each ML's instructional needs and the language resources they can contribute to the class. Here are a few examples of expanded a "language surveys" you can use or adapt to determine how to plan and scaffold your lessons based on this information. Make sure you translate the survey into the ML's primary language, which you can find by looking at the school's *Home Language Survey*.

Pronouncing Names Correctly

Have you ever pronounced a student's name incorrectly? Yeah, me too.

We all realize that correctly pronouncing our Multilingual Learners' names is crucial for trust and community-building. Names are part of a child's identity. Many of us have heard stories where teachers repeatedly mispronounce a student's name or even change it to make it easier for them. This can have a lasting, negative impact on that student. On the other hand, when a

---

2 United States Department of Education

3 García, Ofelia, and Rosario Torres-Guevara. "11 Monoglossic Ideologies and Language Policies in the Education of US Latinas/os." *Handbook of latinos and education: Theory, research, and practice* (2009): 182.

Sample *Expanded* Home Language Survey

Student Name: **Grade:** **Age:**

Date of Arrival to the US: **Languages:**

What language did you learn first?	
What other language(s) have you learned?	
What language(s) do you use with your parents (or adults at your home)?	
What language(s) do you use with your grandparents?	
What language(s) do you use with aunts, uncles, and cousins?	
What language(s) do you use with your siblings (brothers and sisters)?	
I read and write mostly in the following language(s):	
I speak in mostly in the following language(s):	
I watch TV mostly in the following language(s):	
I listen to music mostly in the following language(s):	
The subjects (math, social studies, art, writing, reading, science) I am confident in are:	
How comfortable are you using English? OK in front of entire class? Small groups?	
How often do you read at home in your primary language?	

- What other questions would you add?
- As a content area teacher, why would you want to have this information?
- Other thoughts or insights?

teacher pronounces their students' names correctly, the positive effect is immediately apparent. Often the student smiles in recognition of their name—it helps them feel valued and respected.

I have the best intentions, but sometimes I fail. At the beginning of one school year, I remember asking a student's name and then saying it back to them. Sadly, I saw them grimace and reply, "It's OK, Ms. C-R, you can give me a new English name."

I shook my head. "No, I want to say it right," I insisted.

So, the student repeated it again, and when I said it back to them, it was still off. I could tell by her expression. Ugh.

My own experience lets me know that a teacher might not be able to pronounce a name on their first attempt. Nonetheless, to repeat the name more than a few times in front of the class can be embarrassing for a student. At a time when they are trying to fit in, too much attention is on them.

Over time, I have learned these techniques that might help you:

1. After the student says their name, write it down on a notecard phonetically. Let them know that you are going to practice it.
2. During a break in class, call the student over privately and ask them if you can record them on your phone saying their name so that you can practice it at home. I find this method to be so helpful. I can hear the child saying it with the correct pronunciation and practice on my own to not put undue attention on the student.
3. Instruct all the students to stand in a circle to introduce themselves at the start of a new class. Each student goes around the circle saying something like, "My name is Clara." Then all the students in the class repeat. "Hi, Clara." The group recall exercise helps all the students practice it correctly because they are saying it in unison.

Story Stewardship with Story Circles

At the beginning of most classes I teach, I facilitate story circles. What is a story circle? A story circle is a group of individuals sitting in a circle, sharing stories—usually from their own experience or imagination—focusing on a common theme. Here's an example of how I might implement story circles at the beginning of a class. First, I learn each of my students' names and encourage all class members to do the same (more on that here). I instruct them to write their names on index cards with their pronouns. After that, I invite them to move from the tables to a circle of chairs so there are no back rows and everyone can see each other's faces. I encourage them to share a short story that helps us get to know them. I give them time to think and let them share in whatever order they want. As they express a bit about themselves, I model respectful exchanges by asking questions and looking directly at each person as they talk. These stories elicit emotion: laughter, gasps of surprise, frustration, and even sadness. I encourage the students to make connections with their classmates after they share. My goal for the first day of class is to start developing a classroom community. I explicitly tell them that I want them to interact with each other, not just me.

For middle school students, you might need to create a game to help the stories to flow. A successful middle school teacher I know creates get-to-know-you games such as a bingo card that has ideas such as "Find someone who ________________ (paints, speaks Arabic, eats rice every day, loves video games, etc.)." Another idea is to pass out M&Ms and tell them they can't eat them until the game is done. She then asks an open-ended question and says that everyone who has a red M&M will answer, and so on. Otherwise she says fewer students participate.

Creating a classroom community where the members continually strive to be inclusive is an overarching goal in every course I teach. I intentionally carve out time and carefully plan for brave spaces within each class session. I use the term "brave spaces" rather than "safe spaces" because I believe that no public spaces are truly safe, especially for Multilingual Learners in mainstream classes[4]. It's challenging to speak in a language that is new to you, no matter how outgoing you are in your primary language. Brave spaces are not static. It might mean that students in my class can come together and have difficult conversations by listening to each other, even though that might be challenging and sometimes tense, and sometimes it might mean MLs sit in silence. "Brave spaces" means that we all sometimes sit with discomfort. When MLs are centered through intentional curriculum and contextual teaching where their ways of learning are highlighted, our White, monolingual, English-speaking students might be required to sit in discomfort—so the classroom becomes a place of growth for them.

Many emotions and experiences present the same way. I could observe a student with tears in their eyes and try to guess what they are feeling, but tears could result from a speck of dirt, grief, embarrassment, or frustration. I can't know for sure unless I ask.

Even though research shows that there are some universal facial expressions for a small number of emotions, how each student expresses what they are feeling or thinking and how they experience an event can be as unique as they are.

So why does this matter? A meaningful connection that allows us to learn in community requires that we understand our students—not every single thing every day, but in general, we need to connect with them. It's always easier to connect with someone who is more like us. Teachers have admitted to me that they have the closest relationships with students with similar interests, racial backgrounds, religions, or the same hobby. To connect with students from backgrounds different from ours, we need to be critically conscious or have heightened awareness.

To truly know what students are experiencing, we need to ask them in a respectful way that avoids assumptions. Only then can we connect with confidence to encourage and support them. When our students tell us what they are feeling, what happened, what they fear, and what they desire, and we attentively listen, we can be trusted with their stories and experiences.

---

4 Coles-Ritchie, Marilee, and Robin Renee Smith. "Taking the risk to engage in race talk: Professional development in elementary schools." *International Journal of Inclusive Education* 21.2 (2017): 172–186.

Indigenous scholar Gregory Cajete[5] writes:

> Stories were the first ways humans stored information; they were the basis of the oral tradition of all Tribal peoples. Since the beginning of human history, Tribal cultures have ordered the understanding and meaning of human existence through their remembrance and enactment of stories in ritual, song, dance, and art. Stories have deep roots stemming not only from the physiology and contexting process of the brain but also from the very heart of the human psyche. Stories reflect aspects of the way the human mind organizes and remembers information. At a deeper level, they reflect the topography and language of the human spirit. However, stories go beyond education and the recitation of words. Indigenous stories related the experience of life lived in time, place, and spirit. They were not only a description or narrative but an echo of a truth lived and remembered. They remain the most "*human*" of human forms of communication.

Biographical Surveys

All students come to school with "Funds of Knowledge"[6], but not all schools and classrooms recognize it. While the FoK protocol suggests conducting home visits, that isn't practical or advised for secondary school teachers because they are assigned well over a hundred students a term. One way to understand your students' experiences is to create an assignment with survey questions.

Secondary students are sometimes hesitant to answer some personal questions on a survey, so I suggest creating a list of possible questions and having them choose which they like best. Here's a great list of 101 to get started from Panorama Education[7]:

Interests (choose any three to answer)

- In your free time, what do you like to do?
- Have you volunteered in your community? What have you done?
- What are a few books that have engaged you?
- What do you like to watch on TV or YouTube?
- What are some of your favorite movies?

Emotions (choose any three to answer)

- Which of the following traits do you think best describes you? Funny, thoughtful, caring, outgoing, or ________.
- How do you most like to connect with your friends? Through social media, by talking over

5 Cajete, Gregory A. "Children, myth and storytelling: An Indigenous perspective." *Global Studies of Childhood* 7.2 (2017): 113–130.

6 González, Norma, Luis C. Moll, and Cathy Amanti, eds. *Funds of knowledge: Theorizing practices in households, communities, and classrooms.* Routledge, 2006.

7 www.panoramaed.com/blog/get-to-know-you-questions-for-students

the phone or texting, or by meeting up in person?

- What is one thing your teacher can do to get to know you better?
- What are some things you want me to know about you?
- When you are stressed or anxious, what do you do to relax?
- What makes you feel the most appreciated and understood?
- How would your friends or a relative describe you?

Family and Cultural Background (choose any three to answer)

- What does dinner time look like at your house?
- What are some family items or artifacts that represent your culture and identity?
- Who do you admire in your family?
- What are some happy memories you have with your family or loved ones?
- Describe a member of your family or culture traditions that you like.
- Does your family have pets? If not, would you like to have a pet? What kind?
- What are some of your favorite meals?
- Do you have siblings? What are their names and ages? What do you do for fun with them?

Content-Specific Surveys

It's important to understand how my MLs regard schooling, especially because formal schooling might be very different in their countries. They might have different expectations of teachers, the process of schooling, and assessment. This survey gives me a window into what they enjoy and also what they are accustomed to.

- What is schooling like in your country? How many hours each day were you at school? Where did you sit? What did the teachers do?
- Think about one of your favorite teachers. Describe an activity you did in their class.
- What do you especially like to study?
- What are some topics/areas of study that are most challenging for you?
- How do you study best (quiet, by yourself, with music, etc.)?
- What are some things you would like to do better as a student?
- What do you like most about school?
- What do you like least about school?
- What is something you would really want to learn about at school?
- Which of the following is your favorite way to learn: by talking with others, listening, watching films, or reading? How would you describe yourself as a student? Do you feel you could do better in school or are you satisfied with your performance so far? State all or just choose what works best.

Identity-Concept Maps

Identity-concept maps are a graphic tool that can help students consider the many factors that shape who they are as individuals and how they connect to small and large communities. As Paul

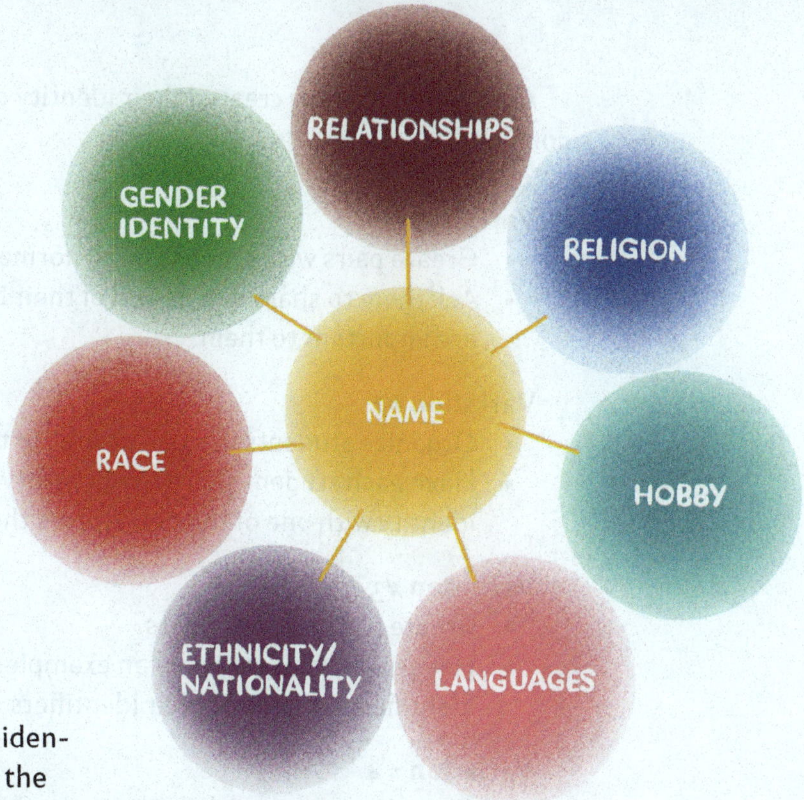

Gorski[8] explains, this activity allows students to explore the multiple dimensions of our identities. The students address the relationships between their desires to self-define identities and the social constructions that label them. I use identity charts to deepen my understanding of my students and help them connect to each other. In turn, the students begin to better understand the many facets of themselves. They see how they connect with large and small societal groups, the school, the community, city, state, and nation. Sharing the identity charts they create with peers can help students build relationships and break down stereotypes. In this way, identity charts can be used as an effective classroom community-building tool.

I usually wait to have students develop concept-identity maps until we've established some trust within the class community. I tell them that they only need to share what they are comfortable sharing with a classmate and me. If they would like, they can share it with the entire class, but that is up to them.

If I ask my students to do a task like this that requires vulnerability, I also do the same. I usually create a map that I project for them to see. The categories may or may not be those that the students choose.

I like the idea of having the class brainstorm identity categories, as they might come up with some that I wouldn't have thought of. You can ask, "What is included in the question Who am I? So many aspects make up the person we are, such as our role in a family (daughter, sister, mother), our hobbies and interests (guitar player, football fan), our religious or spiritual affiliation, our ethnicity, our racial makeup, our gender, our sexual orientation, etc." Our identities sometimes change, while others feel very central to who we are, no matter what. Some of our identities are labels that others put on us that may or may not feel comfortable.

Here are the directions:

- Place your name in the center circle or whatever shape makes sense to you.
- Write an aspect of your identity in each of the satellite circles that you think is an important part of your identity. This can include anything: Asian American, female, daughter, athlete, volleyball player, Buddhist, dog lover, or any descriptor with which you identify.
- At the bottom, complete the following phrase:
  I am (a/an) ____________________ but I also____________________."
  E.g., I am a Buddhist, but I enjoy celebrating Christmas.

---

8 www.paulgorski.org

After students have created their identity circles, there are lots of ways to use them to create community.

Variation #1:

- Create pairs with students who normally do not sit together.
- Ask them to share one or two of their identities with their partner and explain why they are important to them.

Variation #2

- Organize students in small groups of three or four.
- Have each student share a short story about a time they were especially proud to identify with one of the descriptors they used on their wheel.

Variation #3

- Create pairs with students.
- Have each students share an example about a time it was especially difficult to be identified with one of their identifiers or descriptors.

Variation #4

- Organize students in small groups of three or four.
- Have each student name a stereotype associated with one of the groups with which you identify that is not consistent with who they are. They can rely on the sentence they completed or one of their own.

It is often helpful to show students a completed identity chart before they create one of their own. Here's an example:

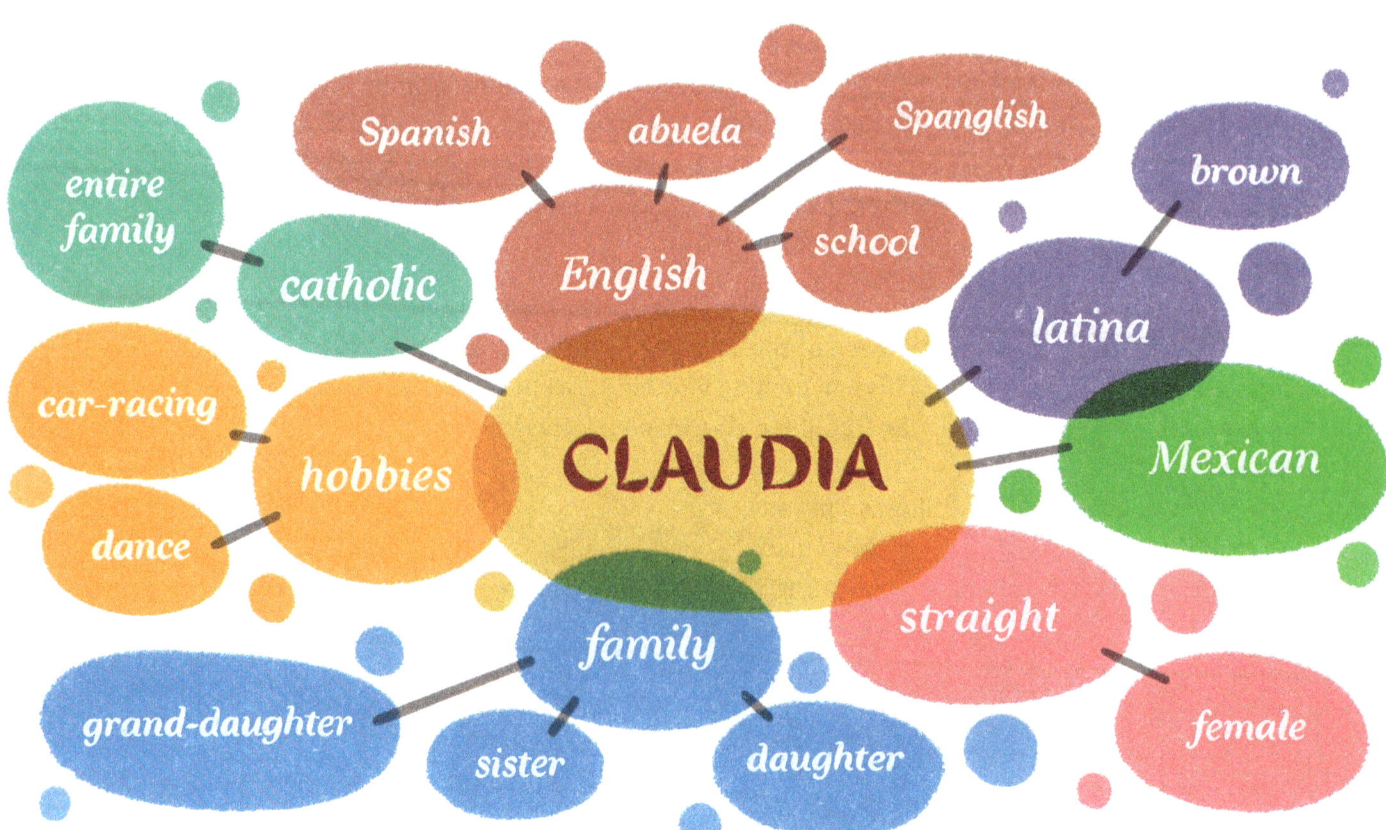

Break-the-Ice Games for Connection

In secondary school settings, we are sometimes reticent to engage in games with our students. We may feel like they are too old or that they'll think we are not respecting their age. Nonetheless, if approached with sensitivity, games can help students really connect with each other. I highly recommend playing games that help students get to know each other.

Here are a few ideas (adapted from *Culturally Responsive Teaching for Multilingual Learners*[9]) that have worked in all kinds of settings—including with adults—so they aren't too young for secondary students.

ROSE, THORN, AND BUD

In this activity, students briefly share something about their day or past week. You can have them think about it or you can provide this simple graphic organizer.

1. Share this graphic organizer on the projector and explain what each element means. Enlarge the graphic if needed.
2. Let students think quietly on their own for a couple of minutes.
3. Instruct students to write their ideas on the graphic organizer or paper in whatever language feels comfortable to them.
4. Share your written ideas with the class.
5. Group students into pairs or threes to share what they wrote down. Since this is a short activity, you can also have them get up and move to different parts of the room.

WHAT I WISH MY TEACHERS KNEW ABOUT ME

Assigning this activity toward the beginning of the year is a great way to get an insider view of what your students want you to know about them. Because this is personal information, you may want to wait a few weeks before asking your students to complete it. Also, make sure you are ready to follow through with the ideas or suggestion your students share. See the handout on the following spread, but you can get more information here: unconditionallearning.org

COMPARE AND CONTRAST WITH PARTNER (VENN DIAGRAM)

For this activity, pair students who might not normally sit together. Together, they create a Venn Diagram that includes their similarities and differences. To support MLs at the beginning stages, you could provide sentence stems such as:

- I love ___________.
- I worry about ___________.
- I have ___________.
- I don't have ___________.
- I would like to ___________.
- I speak ___________.
- I can ___________.

---

9 Snyder, Sydney, and Diane Staehr Fenner. *Culturally responsive teaching for multilingual learners: Tools for equity.* Corwin, 2021.

Rose	Thorn	Bud
(a highlight, success, something good that happened)	(a challenge, disappointment, or something bad that happened)	(new ideas or something you are looking forward to doing)

What I Wish My Teachers Knew About Me

Name:

1.

2.

3.

After students finish, they can present their sentences to the class with a projector. Another idea is to post them around the classroom and give students an opportunity to wander around and read with music playing in the background.

Here's an example:

Exploring Learning Preferences (explain error of learning styles)

Educators have debunked the notion that people have certain learning styles. The word "style," by definition, means "a particular way of doing something," so a "learning style" implies a stable, consistent, or static way of learning across all tasks and settings. That's almost never the case. An individual's learning preferences vary, depending on the subject, the nature of the task, others participating in the activity (including the teacher), and much more. This is important to remember, because you don't want to put students in boxes ("that student is a visual learner") and only teach to their strengths. Nonetheless, it's useful to understand their learning preferences for some activities, especially because they most likely attended schools that look different from their current one. Creating an activity where students think about and share their learning preferences can inform your instructional decisions. At times you may want to allow them choices that support those preferences, and pay attention to whether you are teaching to the majority English primary speakers or the preferences of your MLs. Other ideas that might be useful are asking if they prefer working in groups, pairs, or individually, or if they like working in silence or with music.

See an example on the next page.

Learning Preference Survey

I learn best ...	Always	Sometimes	Never	Explain!
with a partner				
in a small group				
by myself				
with hands-on work				
sitting in the front				
in my primary language				
when I can see examples				
when I sit still				
when I can move around				
with visuals (pictures, films, demos)				

Seating

In the content section, we'll talk more about how to group students. I would make it a habit to move students around so that they naturally get to know other students in the class. If that is done regularly, the students won't view it as a punishment. Also, if you engage in group work throughout the class period, they'll realize that they will have a chance to sit by their friends, too.

Smash It

Lorean Escota Germán wrote a fabulous book called *Textured Teaching*[10] where she outlines a variety of ways to create a classroom where all can express themselves. One idea that is simple but effective in letting students know that they can also share negative emotions is *Smash It*.

Students write what they are most frustrated about or what bothers them about the school or classroom community. When you say to "go", all the students can crumple up their pieces of paper and throw it at the white board. Call on a couple of students to pick up all the papers and jot down the ideas on the board.

Decide as a class community which one of those on the "problems" on the board they want to address. Use translation for the words through a device or another students who is bilingual. Have students brainstorm in small groups how they might problem solve.

Connecting with Multilingual Learners Outside the Classroom

CLUBS

Connecting with students often happens outside the classroom. I realize the lives of secondary teachers are already full and districts are asking you to do more and more, but if at all possible, volunteer to be the faculty sponsor for clubs that support MLs (e.g., Black Student Union, Amnesty International, Language Clubs, Immigrant Rights, etc.). And if you already run, for example, the Robotics Club, a sports team, or Key Club, make sure you invite your ML students to join. A personal invitation is just what they might need to feel like they belong. If your school doesn't have clubs that appeal to MLs in your classrooms, encourage your students to start one and agree to be the sponsor.

FIELD TRIPS

Planning field trips that align with your content area is a great way to add context and connection to your students' understanding of course goals. Seeing a play, going to a river, observing works of art at a museum, or visiting a robotics lab can prompt questions, interest, and a ____ of a subject matter. While visits are difficult logistically, parents, alumni associations, and administrators are often willing to help make these outside experiences possible for your students. While you are off campus, students will often open up and share more to allow for a greater understanding of life experience and connection.

---

10 Germán, Lorena Escoto. *Textured teaching: A framework for culturally sustaining practices*. Heinemann, 2021.

If field trips are not feasible due to parent permission and cost, I would recommend virtual fieldtrips. You can look at Discovery Education and other sites to do this. One middle school teacher reported creating different stations in class where students attend "field trips" to study different places such as Anne Frank's house, concentration camp tours, and more.

COMMUNITY WALKS

I appreciate spending time in communities where MLs and their communities live and work. By spending time in these neighborhoods, I have learned more about their experiences with food, religion, spirituality, music, employment, and a variety of cultural arts. Whenever I have enjoyed a meal at one of the local restaurants, visited a local church congregation, or participated in a community center activity, I have engaged in conversations that give me more insight into what my students' value and how I might use what I have learned in what I teach. I also learn about what contributions these communities might be able to make and what struggles they face, so that schools might construct support systems.

Here's a list of ideas:

- Visit a house of worship
- Attend a community event
- Shop at a local grocery store
- Dine in a restaurant owned by an ML family
- Walk around the neighborhood right before or after the elementary school lets out

All families and communities are rich resources that can contribute to your classroom. Here are some tips on how to build that relationship:

1. Create routines and possibly homework accessible for MLs' parents or guardians through translating them and possibly providing a hard copy rather than only electronic.
2. Consider inviting communities to your classroom to highlight student work such as a mini science fair, slam poetry events, concerts, or art fairs. One middle school example is a Multilingual Learner night for students and families. We provide dinner and games, then show parents how to use all the school online programs such as Canvas and Skyward. We try to do this in August or September, and it has been a huge help in getting to know our families.
3. Let parents/guardians know that you are their partner in supporting their child's academic success. One teacher sends the families postcards, which has also been a huge way to connect with them. I try to send twelve postcards a term to let parents know how well their students are doing, or to tell them something I really enjoy about their students. It is quick and easy, and most schools will pay for the postage.
4. Call guardians/parents to update them on successes, not just when there are problems. There are free online programs such as "Talking Points" that let teachers text families in their home language. This has been super valuable, since everyone has a phone and reads their texts.

Creating Joy

Finally, strive to create a classroom of joy. This idea was explored in depth by author Gouldy Muhammad[11] in her book *Unearthing Joy*. I highly recommend it for lots of general practices for the K–12 classroom. In the beginning, she suggests that teachers ask themselves the following questions which I have adapted about joy in their classrooms.

- How do you define joy?
- What is an experience from your K–12 classroom that brought joy?
- How often was joy centered in your teacher preparation classes?
- How is your classroom rich with joy?
- How do you see joy in the curriculum you teach?
- How can you cultivate joy among you and your students?

To her point, we often concentrate on the heaviness of the world and the problems that need to be overcome in education. As such, we need to invite joy into our classrooms to alleviate the tension and stress that is often present. This is especially important for MLs so that the process of language acquisition contains laughter and silliness.

11 Muhammad, Gholdy, et al. *Unearthing joy: A guide to culturally and historically responsive curriculum and instruction.* Scholastic Inc, 2023.

CHAPTER THREE

Context for Content

3

"If you're talking all the time, how can you hear the impact of your teaching?"

— JOHN HATTIE

Some years ago, I walked into a small stucco building in Cuenca, Ecuador, to teach an after-school "English as a Foreign Language" class to teenagers. My supervisor was going to observe me that day and I was a bit nervous but excited to demonstrate the activities I had planned. Students sat in a semi-circle and cooperatively engaged in the pair/share games when they weren't listening to me.

After the class, my supervisor asked me a question: "How much do you think you talked, and how much do you think the students talked?"

I made a guess of about 20 percent for me and 80 percent for the students. She said she timed me and it was more like 60 percent for me and 40 percent for them.

"Is that what you want?" she asked.

Aghast, I said absolutely not. That was a pivotal moment in my teaching, and from then on I intentionally planned for way more open but structured talk time for my students.

Chapter Three focuses on the important of context in language learning. Students need to be able to "see" what they are learning. Dr. James Cummins, an often-cited bilingual educator and researcher, created a graph as a guideline for teachers when planning curriculum. He introduced the concepts of BICS and CALP that have been critiqued by some researchers but can be a helpful starting guide for content teachers as they begin to think about how they can make their lessons more contextual.

BICS (Basic Interpersonal Communication Skills) is social-situation language. BICS is used on the playground, at dinner, at the grocery store, or between two friends in conversation. BICS usually involves context-embedded and meaningful situations that are less demanding in terms of cognitive capacity. Because BICS involves vocabulary and grammar that are often repeated in informal speech, it comes more easily. But as we all know, sometimes social situations can be more stressful than academic settings, depending on many factors.

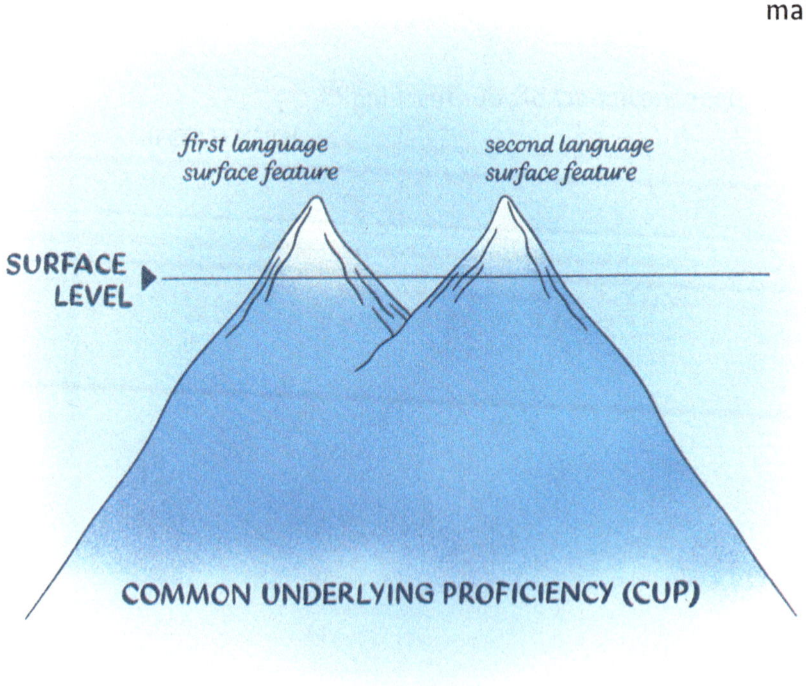

CALP (Cognitive Academic Language Proficiency) refers to more formal interactions around subject-area contents in the classroom. CALP development initiates from birth but separates from BICS after school starts; social context of schooling is its specific feature. CALP includes academic language used to compare and contrast, categorize, synthesize, evaluate, and infer. CALP is a more specialized language (Cummins, 1981[1]).

So basically, Cummins's 2008 iceberg model (CUP) of bilingualism shows how languages can transfer cognitive and literacy skills. In the image shown

1 Cummins, Jim. *Bilingualism and Minority-Language Children. Language and Literacy Series.* The Ontario Institute for Studies in Education, 1981.

here, two icebergs represent two languages, but they infer more overlap. Both icebergs share a common underlying system of knowledge with the water as their deep structure; they share similar concepts even though both languages are separate.

This graphic illuminates language acquisition and the importance of encouraging MLs to use all their linguistic repertoires. As students are in the process of language acquisition, they develop a metalinguistic knowledge that supports acquisition in other languages. Why was this theory important to Cummins? He wanted to show that cognitive academic skills increase through cross-lingual proficiencies. By demonstrating the interdependence of concepts, skills, and linguistic knowledge found in a central processing system, he hoped that teachers would encourage multilingualism by drawing on the primary language of their students, even if it wasn't English. When they learned a concept in one language, it would benefit the second or third language. His research was and still is essential for teachers to understand the academic language acquisition process and provides evidence that drawing on languages other than English when teaching subject-specific material is effective.

Learning happens when students are asked to engage in activities that are beyond a learner's ability but with high support to meet the challenge. So why did Cummins teach BICS and CALP? Many teachers of MLs were erroneously confusing a child's fast development with BICS in the classroom with the often more time-consuming language acquisition of CALP. They heard MLs chatting pretty fluently with their friends and assumed that their level of English development in their specific content area was higher than it was. Thus, they didn't "scaffold" or shelter the language for them and wondered why they were not progressing in the classroom. I don't fault the teachers for this, as there is a lack of ongoing professional development for secondary teachers for working with MLs. Cummins (1986)[2] explained, "Failure to take account of the BICS/CALP (conversational/academic) distinction has resulted in discriminatory psychological assessment of bilingual students and premature exit from language support programs (e.g. bilingual education in the United States) into mainstream classes" (p. 24). Exit into mainstream classes that do little to create spaces for their ML students results in limited progress and even contributes to push-out rates. Cummins[3] has reviewed linguistic practices for MLs in his most recent book.

On the next page you'll see a chart of typical tasks in secondary schools. Each task is placed in a quadrant that represents high/context embedded support or low/context reduced support and high or low challenging tasks.

The goal is to stay in the B zone as much as possible. In this zone, MLs are challenged with higher-order thinking, but they are also supported contextually through interactions, graphics, translanguaging, and high-quality curriculum that connects to their lived life experiences.

I have categorized the ideas of content into teacher direct instruction with active participation and student-to-student interaction. The teacher's direct instruction should be short, contextual, and embedded with student engagement. Interaction is where the students interact with each other to go deeper with the content you presented. Content sharing and interaction are a part

---

2 Cummins, Jim. "Empowering minority students: A framework for intervention." *Harvard educational review* 56.1 (1986): 18-37.

3 Cummins, Jim. Rethinking the education of multilingual learners: A critical analysis of theoretical concepts. Vol. 19. *Multilingual Matters*, 2021.

Multilingual Learner Support Quadrant

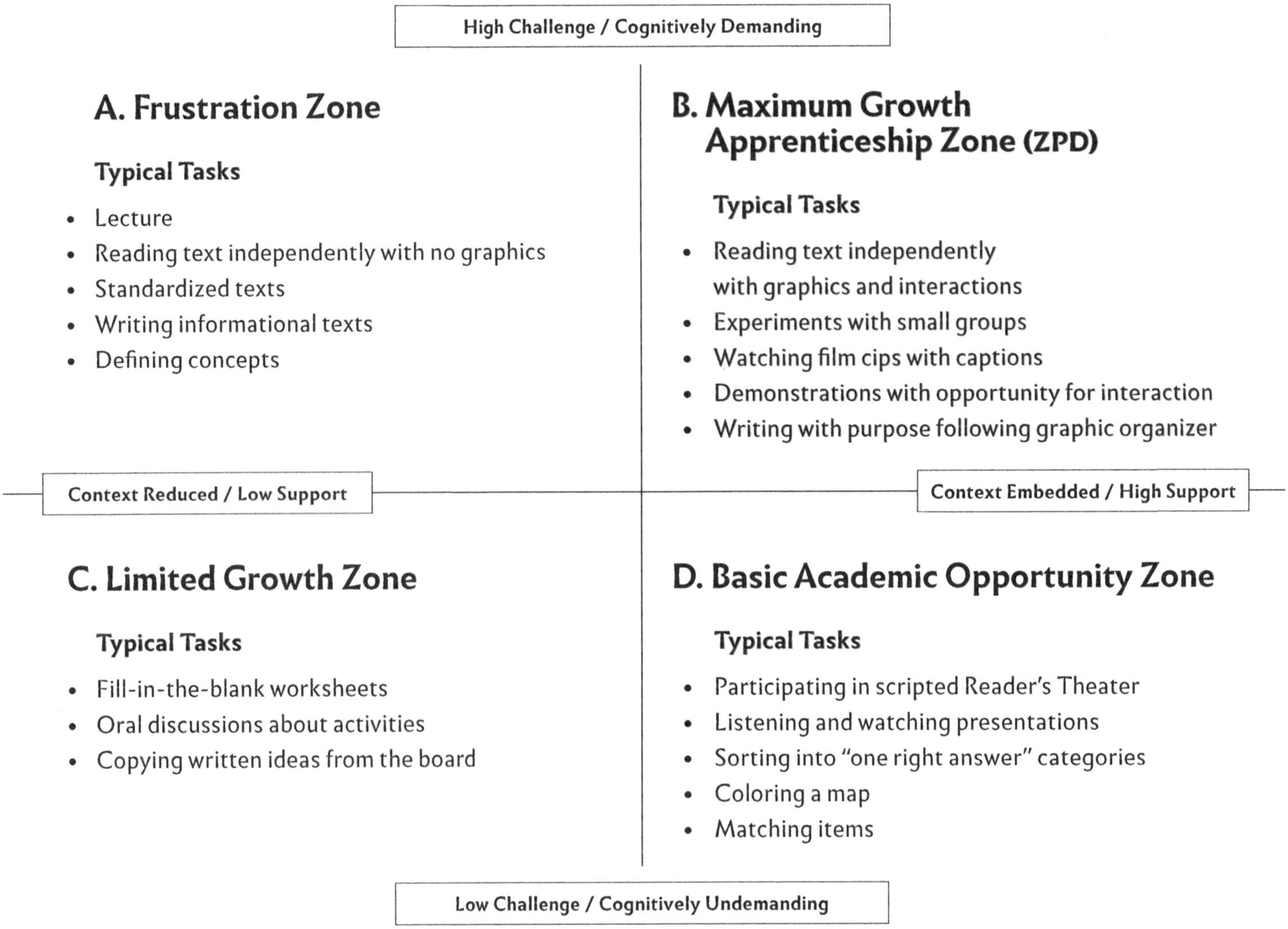

High Challenge / Cognitively Demanding

A. Frustration Zone

Typical Tasks

- Lecture
- Reading text independently with no graphics
- Standardized texts
- Writing informational texts
- Defining concepts

B. Maximum Growth Apprenticeship Zone (ZPD)

Typical Tasks

- Reading text independently with graphics and interactions
- Experiments with small groups
- Watching film cips with captions
- Demonstrations with opportunity for interaction
- Writing with purpose following graphic organizer

Context Reduced / Low Support

Context Embedded / High Support

C. Limited Growth Zone

Typical Tasks

- Fill-in-the-blank worksheets
- Oral discussions about activities
- Copying written ideas from the board

D. Basic Academic Opportunity Zone

Typical Tasks

- Participating in scripted Reader's Theater
- Listening and watching presentations
- Sorting into "one right answer" categories
- Coloring a map
- Matching items

Low Challenge / Cognitively Undemanding

of every lesson and you might go back and forth with each. For example, you might make a five-minute, context-embedded presentation on molecules with a graphic organizer for your students and then have students talk in pairs about what they wrote on the graphic organizer.

Adapted Text

Academic texts can be overwhelming to new speakers of English. Since the goal is to help students comprehend the goals or standards, manipulating text and other resource materials so it's more accessible can help MLs reach the goal of understanding the most relevant material.

Probably the most important goal is to summarize the text to focus on the key points of

Scaffold Self-Assessment for Instruction

Scaffold	Do not know how to use this scaffold	Understand this scaffold but don't use it regularly	I find this an effective scaffold and use it often
Adapted texts and/or audio texts			
English and/or bilingual glossaries			
Graphic organizers			
Limit teacher talk			
Manipulatives			
Pre-teach vocabulary			
Provide specific background knowledge			
Repeat & paraphrase			
Sentence and Paragraph Frames & Stems			
Translanguaging			
Student-generated visuals			
Cloze notes			

Adapted from Culturally Responsive Teaching for MLs: Tools for Equity information through an outline, list of bulleted points, or graphic organizer. If you are fortunate enough to have an extra helper in your class such as a student aide, paraprofessional, or more-capable peers, enlist them to do this for you.

Ideas to keep in mind:

- Decide what MLs need to learn from the text (focus on the standards or essential question)
- Focus on concrete concepts first, then abstract
- Reduce nonessential details
- Relate new information to students' experiences
- Use visual representations: maps, charts, timelines, outlines
- Simplify vocabulary but keep key concepts and technical terms
- Elaborate to explain concepts if necessary

As I am writing this list, I am thinking, as you might, *who has time to adapt every text I assign to my students?*

Here is a website that can help you: Rewordify [rewordify.com].
Rewordify is free online software. You're using it now — there's nothing to buy or install. It works on any computer, tablet, or smartphone. Just visit "rewordify.com" in your browser and start reading and learning. Also, it is tablet-friendly — no mouse needed. Your class or the entire school can create teacher and student accounts without entering any personal information. The site can help with the following:

1. Intelligently simplify difficult English, for faster comprehension.
2. Effectively teach words, for building a better vocabulary.
3. Help teachers save time and produce engaging lessons.

Develop Oracy

Developing oracy is creating space where MLs can practice articulating ideas, developing understanding of core content, and engaging with others through spoken language. The idea is for teachers to plan lessons that include both learning to talk and learning *through talk*[4]. This term emphasizes the importance of developing students' oral skills in tandem with literacy as they both develop academic connection.

Research shows that MLs gain expertise in literacy in English as their oral proficiency develops, as oracy and literacy are reinforcing[5]. Unfortunately, some research shows that MLs spend less than 2 percent of their time in classrooms in oral interaction[6].

Graunt and Stott claim that oracy contributes to social equity by:

- Increased engagement in content goals

---

4 Gaunt, Amy, and Alice Stott. *Transform teaching and learning through talk: the oracy imperative.* Rowman & Littlefield, 2018.

5 Riches, Caroline, and Fred Genesee. "Literacy: Crosslinguistic and crossmodal issues." *Educating English language learners: A synthesis of research evidence* (2006): 64-108.

6 Soto-Hinman, Ivannia. "Increasing Academic Oral Language Development: Using English Language Learner Shadowing in Classrooms." *Multicultural Education* 18.2 (2011): 21-23.

- Stronger academic achievement
- Improved sense of well-being and confidence
- A sense of belonging and community
- Access to post-secondary opportunities
- Desire for civic and social engagement

With all these positive outcomes, it makes sense to create as many structured interactions in classroom as possible to help facilitate growth. I've shared a few here.

Limit Teacher Talk

Mohr and Mohr[7] explain that research indicates that teacher talk dominates classroom communication. Most teachers are talking for 76 percent of classroom time. Teachers are communicating explanations, questions, commands, modeling, and feedback. Unfortunately, 60 percent of teacher talk involves asking questions that have only one right answer. All students are put on the spot when this happens and MLs are less likely than ever to respond.

Scaffolding Student Responses with Formulaic Expressions

Formulaic expressions are similar to sentence frames, but they emphasize the value of students' unique responses rather than predictable one-word or short phrases. The formulaic expressions support the students as they create the responses. The following tables have language to help you and your MLs, but of course they can be adapted to fit your content and way of speaking. The underlying goal of the charts is to create more emphasis on ML talk and to establish a community in which students are respected and accountable. This modeling allows all students to know that you want to hear from them; even if it takes a bit more time or scaffolding, it is worth it to hear all students' perspectives.

In addition, this language works to enhance students' language and conceptual knowledge. The more students in the class see that you want MLs to respond and know that they have meaningful contributions, the more they'll also respect their contributions in small groups and other settings. You will set a pattern that will become the norm in the classroom community. During whole-class and small-group discussions, you can illicit responses and provide feedback in meaningful and supportive ways. The following tables adapted from Mohr and Mohr's article on Extending English Language Learners' interactions by providing specific examples on how to do that as a teacher.

---

7 Mohr, Kathleen AJ, and Eric S. Mohr. "Extending English-language learners' classroom interactions using the Response Protocol." *The Reading Teacher* 60.5 (2007): 440-450.

TABLE 1

Examples of teacher elaborations of responses that support the content

- You're right! Can you tell me more?
- Yes, that works. What else do you know about ____?
- I have heard that too. How did you learn that?
- That's an insightful answer. Can you also tell me why this ______ is important?
- I appreciate that thinking and the way you expressed it.

TABLE 2

Examples of teacher elaboration of partially correct answers

- Thanks for that response. Can you tell me more?
- Yes, I agree with _____. Let's think more about _____.
- You are telling me some important things about ____, now let's go more into _______.
- We're heading in a direction that gets at our essential question. Do you or does anyone else have something else to add?

TABLE 3

Examples of teacher elaboration when responses are in languages other than English

- All right. That sounds really interesting. How can we say that in English?
- Do you know any words in English to say that?
- Call on someone else in the classroom to say what you said in English. Everyone should hear your thinking.
- Let's translate what you said into English using Google Translate.

TABLE 4

Examples of teacher responses to student questions

- Thank you for asking. Scholars ask a lot of questions.
- Thank you for asking that question.
  I bet others in the class are wondering about that too.
- Wow. What an important question!
  What can help us answer that question?
- Before I give my response, can someone else answer (name of student)'s question?

TABLE 5

Examples of teacher elaborations of incorrect or confusing responses

- Help me understand what you mean. Tell me again.
- I think I heard ______. Is that right?
- Tell me more so I know what you are thinking.
- Do you think _____ or ______?
  (Provide a short menu of options to help give more context.)

TABLE 6

Examples of teacher elaborations in response to student silence

- I think you know something about this. Feel free to tell us in (name of language) and we'll translate it.
- Can you help us know what you are saying by drawing it out?
- Let's have everyone share ideas with the person sitting next to you and I'll call on a few of you after.

ANCHOR CHART FOR AVOIDING THE "IDK" RESPONSE

Ideas for students to say in response to teacher or peers in small groups

- I need a bit more time to think.
- Could you repeat the question?
- Where can I find the information?
- Can you write the question on the board, please?
- I'm not sure, but I think it's _______
- Can we talk in pairs first?
- Can you give me a bit more information?
- What does the word or phrase "____" mean?

All content areas have specific terms and ways of writing unique to that discipline. Scientific literacy is particularly challenging for MLs—as well as dominant English speakers who have had less exposure to academic English. Learning science as a new language involves a focus on vocabulary, but it's more than just memorizing words[8]. Once they learn target vocabulary, MLs need to know how to use the terms to describe the scientific processes they observe[9]. For written and video examples[10] of vocabulary development, check out: Core Practices for Teaching Multilingual Students by Megan Peercy[11] and colleagues. They have a book and a you tube channel with students and teachers in action. Science papers and textbooks often use sentence structures that differ from other written material. This can be challenging for new learners as they read science papers and textbooks and as they are learning to write scientific papers and reports. Because MLs often comprehend more than they can express in English, educators need to be creative in the way they assess their knowledge. One way to add support is to scaffold students' language development by providing them with "sentence frames" for commonly used scientific language functions. California Science Project[12] developed the following list of "sample scientific discourse patterns."

8 Wessels, Stephanie. "Science as a second language: Integrating science and vocabulary instruction for English language learners." (2013).

9 Rodríguez, Diane, Angela Carrasquillo, and Kyung Soon Lee. *The bilingual advantage: Promoting academic development, biliteracy, and native language in the classroom.* Teachers College Press, 2014.

10 Core practices for MLs You Tube Channel. youtube.com/@corepracticesformlls

11 Peercy, Megan Madigan, Johanna M. Tigert, and Daisy E. Fredricks. *Core practices for teaching multilingual students: Humanizing pedagogies for equity.* Teachers College Press, 2023.

12 californiascienceproject.ucr.edu

Sample Scientific Discourse Patterns

Scientific Language Functions	Sentence Structure Frames
Sequence	We saw that first, then, ______________, and at the end, ______________.
Hypothesis	If ______________ had ______________, then ______________ would have ______________.
Identify Relationships	This ______________ is necessary for ______________ because it ______________.
Compare	This ______________ is similar to that ______________ because both ______________.
Contrast	This ______________ is different from that ______________ because one has ______________ and the other doesn't have ______________.
Estimate	Looking at the ______________, I think there are ______________.
Disagree	I don't think the evidence supports ______________ because ______________. I don't agree with that statement because ______________.

**Table adapted from Dobb (2005)*

Too often MLs become passive in mainstream classes because language and cultural differences are disconnecting. When you encourage contributions from them by building context, emphasizing the key components, and rephrasing structures depending on their proficiency, they will be more active participants in whole group and small group discussions.

The takeaways adapted from[13]:

- Expect student participation from all students, including MLs. During key discussions, notice who is participating and who isn't. Avoid hand-raising for participation and instead use think/pair/share, then call on students after they have had time to formulate their ideas.
- Model behaviors that value and elaborate MLs' contributions. Acknowledge their contributions and allow for lots of different ways to express their ideas visually or in their primary language.

---

13 Gibbons, Pauline. *Scaffolding language, scaffolding learning.* Portsmouth, NH: Heinemann, 2002.

- Allow sufficient wait time, including patient pauses that support MLs' possible need for code switching (i.e., thinking or speaking in one language and switching to another). Repeating the question or prompt allows more time for processing while engaging more students.
- Use "yes or no," "either," or other prompts to bridge language at the varying pruriency levels. Oral language production most often follows reception skills, so most MLs can comprehend more than they can say. Giving students a way to show their knowledge without having to construct complete sentences keeps students involved and scaffolds their use of English to evidence their understanding.
- Accept phrases and partial answers. Helping MLs elaborate their ideas into full sentences with academic structures and terms will help them write their ideas in more standard English.
- Speak with a regular speed but add more natural pauses; speaking loudly or super slowly is not necessary. Rephrasing and gesturing can convey meaning.
- Find time to connect casually one to one as much as you can. Ask questions frequently and listen carefully to student responses. Making time for less intimidating exchanges (e.g., small groups, individual conferences) may provide information you can use when leading whole-group discussions later.
- Be an active listener by focusing on the content of the message rather than its grammatical structure. Acknowledging a student's message is likely to increase interaction, while correcting grammar may not—and, in fact, might shift the focus from content to form. It is especially embarrassing to do this in front of the class.
- Learn some key phrases from MLs' home language(s) to make a connection and to show that you are willing to share in the language-learning process. They will be less intimidated when they see you make mistakes too.

Oral Development Jigsaw

I learned this task at a recent QTEL (Quality Teaching of English Learners) professional development conference. It's similar to a reading jigsaw, but focuses on oracy. This activity could be used in any content area to support learning a specific concept.

Step 1: Think/Pair/Share

Think

It's easy to forget this step so you might want to set a timer for a couple of minutes and keep silent so students really have time to think.

Sample Prompt:

- What is a story that you love to listen to and/or tell?
- What makes it such a good story?

Pair/Share

Make sure you have a system for having students work in partners to share or create a chart to project, with all their names in pairs.

With your partner:

- Quickly share the story and also reflect on what you think makes it a good story in whatever language you are comfortable sharing. Use an electronic translation tool if needed.
- Remember: When we share to the class, share what your partner said. Remember to take a few notes to help you.

Step 2:

Arrange students into heterogenous groups of four. You will assign a different color to each child in the group.

Sample chart to show groups:

Oracy Development Jigsaw

EACH STUDENT IS ASSIGNED A DIFFERENT COLOR

Base Groups (heterogenous)

Base Group A	**Base Group B**
Base Group C	**Base Group D**

Step 3:

Tell all the blues to move to the Blue Expert Group, red to the Red Expert Group, etc. They'll be with classmates who all have the same color. Try to keep the groups to three to four students.

BECOME EXPERTS IN DESCRIBING THE ILLUSTRATION

Move to Expert Groups (same color)

Blue Expert Group	**Red Expert Group**
Green Expert Group	**Yellow Expert Group**

Step 4:

All students will be in an "expert" group and each will become an expert in describing the picture. Together, all the students will describe the picture you give them in detail, with no speculation or inference. They can only say words and phrases that they actually see. They should all help everyone in the group to become an expert.

Let the students know that at the next step, they will be the only person who has the information from this picture so they need to take notes and pay attention. They will not have the picture in front of them. (It helps to give students a note card so they have the scaffolding of jotting down ideas.)

Give the students this chart to help scaffold as they ask questions and share ideas.

Language Guide (remember that you can't infer or speculate)

What you can ask	What you can say
Where does the scene take place?	This scene takes place . . .
What people are included in this image?	This image shows . . .
How are the people dressed?	The people are . . .
What are the people doing?	I see . . .
Are there objects in the image? What do they look like?	I notice . . .
Anything else to describe?	I also notice . . .

Step 5:

Instruct the students to go back to their base group, where each person in the group has a different color. In the base group, each person will share descriptions of the picture you gave them.

Let them know that these are the phrases they can use:

- My picture showed . . .
- In my picture, we saw . . .

After descriptions are complete, you may ask questions of each other.

Sequence the four images in whichever way makes sense to you for the story you are going to create. Encourage the students to be imaginative and rely on their linguistic repertoire.

- Be creative and imaginative as you narrate and breathe life into your story! (Also, each participant should keep their own written copy of the shared story.)
- If time, rehearse narrating your story, with everyone participating, taking turns by following the order you decided upon for the images
- Walqui and Lier encourage teachers to design appropriate scaffolding structures and processes like this that support student's participation in extended interactions. What else support can you add that allows them to talk longer. Here are some tips:
- Integrate oracy and literacy together.
- Create meaningful purposes for communication and a variety of opportunities to use language in context.
- Apprentice students into disciplinary practices by supporting them to move from peripheral (but legitimate) participation to appropriation.

Videos with Closed Caption

Videos are a contextual way to present material to MLs. Short videos are available for a wide variety of content and can add an element of humor, graphic representative, and depth. This visually engaging content often shows how English is used in real-world situations, which can bring the ideas you are trying to convey to life.

Conveniently, YouTube and other videos can be embedded in web pages and on Canvas or other teacher sites. These include animated songs, informative videos, and clips from drama and documentaries in English and other languages. When captions are enabled, MLs are able to hear in English, see the visuals, and also see the words that match the audio. It makes understanding the content easier. Of course, for students at the beginning stages of language acquisition, you might need to enable the captions in their primary language(s). Dello and Linder explain that turning on closed captioning when showing video content improved student learning not only for MLs but also for students with learning disabilities.

Visuals

Visuals are one of the most useful ways to create comprehension for MLs. A visual can be anything that students can look at to help them comprehend content that you share. One of the premier language-learning linguists, Stephen Krashen, coined the concept "comprehensible input." Some examples of visuals in a presentation could be charts, physical gestures, digital or printed images, and illustrations of vocabulary. I have seen teachers create comprehensible input with PowerPoint presentations by limiting text on each slide and inserting images that illustrate the content. I suggest using more slides with less text (24+ point font) and more images or graphics.

Translation Tools

Voice typing and translation tools are also examples of text-based visual aids that help teach MLs. Voice-to-text application tools can assist students who might be confident in their vocabulary but are at the beginning stages of spelling and writing development in English. MLs can participate in mainstream content area courses with more engagement when translation tools are readily available. They can more quickly assimilate unfamiliar concepts to their schema.

Visual Aids (Student-Generated)

I indicated earlier that it's important to economize your time in integrating context into your content area. Incorporating student-created visuals into the lesson not only saves you time, it can also help other students learn the material in a deeper way. MLs can benefit from self-created visual aids to recall and transfer knowledge. As students express themselves artistically, they add deeper understanding of the content into their mental models. Students also learn from each other as the visuals they create might be more connecting than something a publishing company or teacher might produce, because of shared interests and age. Activities such as drawing and performing can not only aid in student comprehension, they can also give students an accessible outlet for demonstrating their understanding.

Student-Generated Dictionaries

Each content area has its own specialized vocabulary, so I recommend having all students in your course, especially MLs, create a dictionary. This can be as simple as buying a small notebook and adding tabs from A–Z. When students come across vocabulary they are unfamiliar with, they write the word, a definition in their own words, and draw a small picture to help them remember it. The dictionaries are tailored to each student—they only add the content-specific vocabulary words they don't know.

Students learn best from their personal experiences. As children are writing, they need to know how to look up words in the dictionary. Standard dictionaries have so many words, it can be challenging for MLs to use the dictionary effectively. Since the ideas in their student dictionary are self-generated, students are more inclined to use their dictionaries.

Experiments/Demonstration

(You'll find more about group work where students produce experiments in Chapter Four.)

Implementing experiments and hands-on learning are natural ways for MLs to learn content and interact with peers in a comfortable way. It's useful to demonstrate an experiment in front of the class, as they provide lots of visual comprehensible input.. To create more comprehensible input, label each item you are using, pause for emphasis, and ask an assistant to write key ideas on the board. Students could have a graphic organizer with the experiment steps on a hand-out.

Graphic Organizers

A few years ago, I went to a conference focused on strategies for Multilingual Learners. I presented on the value of graphic organizers, and the response was overwhelming. Teachers were drawn to this pedagogical tool that has been around since the 1980s because it is so effective for engaging students and comprehending content. A **graphic organizer** is also known as a **concept map, story map, cognitive organizer, advance organizer,** or **concept diagram** that uses visual symbols to express knowledge and concepts through relationships between them.

Research has shown the effectiveness of graphic organizers, especially for MLs, as the information is organized in a visual way, making it easier to understand and learn key vocabulary. Fortunately, a plethora of websites have graphic organizers that are ready to print or manipulate to fit your specific objectives. Choosing a graphic organizer that mirrors the material is key. For some concepts, such as the overlap between wetlands and marshes, a Venn diagram might work best, while for understanding chronological steps in history, a timeline makes more sense.

Here are some underlying principles to consider:

- Verbalize the relationship between the ideas and the information that will be taught by projecting the graphic organizer so it's easy to see. Demonstrate what a student might add to the graphic organizer through presenting information through a "think aloud," where you say out loud what you are thinking and then write it down in the appropriate spot on the graphic organizer. Graphic organizers should be tailored to reinforce the relationships between concepts, reminding students that this is just a quick preview of the material that will be taught next.
- As you are presenting the material on the graphic organizer, provide opportunities for students to participate in discussions. In order to participate, MLs need to have numerous pauses to process language.
- Once students have the opportunity to share their thoughts and understand the topic that will follow, teachers can start to connect new material to their prior knowledge. Lessons need to guide MLs to activate prior knowledge as they recollect content taught earlier to be able to retain new material.
- In other words, graphic organizers provide a visual summary as they describe information, introducing MLs to new technical vocabulary as they reinforce decoding skills of key words for an upcoming lesson.

Graphic organizers facilitate MLs' comprehension through visual illustrations of key terms, vocabulary, ideas, and the relationships between them. Improving reading comprehension can be challenging, especially in content areas with new concepts and more technical vocabulary. Graphic organizers can provide a place to organize essential material without overwhelming beginning learners with too much information. It's essential to model how to use graphic organizers for MLs. This can be through a "think aloud" on a projector or by creating small groups with a facilitator who can explain them at each table. Circulate the room to check on students for clarity after the session beings.

On the following pages are a few examples of graphic organizers that are commonly used in every content area.

K-W-L-Q

Topic:

Name(s):

What do you know?	What do you want to know?	What did you learn?	What questions do you still have?

Persuasion Writing Graphic Organizer

Name:

Main Idea

Reason #1	Reason #2	Reason #3
Facts & Examples	Facts & Examples	Facts & Examples
Facts & Examples	Facts & Examples	Facts & Examples
Facts & Examples	Facts & Examples	Facts & Examples
Facts & Examples	Facts & Examples	Facts & Examples
Facts & Examples	Facts & Examples	Facts & Examples
Facts & Examples	Facts & Examples	Facts & Examples
Facts & Examples	Facts & Examples	Facts & Examples

Translanguaging

Translanguaging encourages Multilingual Learners' full linguistic repertoire, instead of trying to keep narrowly focused on a single language, which is primarily English in the United States[14]. I got to hear Ofelia Garcia speak in person at a QTEL conference recently, and this idea resonated with me: MLs do not have two or three buckets with different languages. Instead, they do language with extended repertoire of linguistic and multimodal features. Therefore, translanguaging is a unitary repertoire. She emphasized that our students who are learning English are not simply ELLs (English language learners)—they are emergent plurolinguals who are always emerging.

When I first started teaching ESL (English as a Second Language), as it was inaccurately called, we were highly encouraged to only allow our students to speak English. More research has informed us that forbidding students to use their primary* (i.e., home, heritage, native) languages in schools can impede their understanding of key content material. Highlighting the cognitive benefits of multilingualism is something to share not only with MLs but also with students who grew up monolingually, because of the stigma surrounding learners in the process of learning English. Too often in schools, MLs are most often prohibited from using all their resources.

** I prefer the term "primary language" over "home" or "native" because a primary language is that with which a multilingual speaker has greatest proficiency, even if it isn't their heritage or native language.*

Cutting-edge research informs us that MLs can use their primary language to transfer their knowledge and understanding into English. Even if you don't speak the primary languages of your students, there are many ideas you can implement. By opening up translanguaging spaces for strategic reasons to match how MLs "do" language, their dynamic translanguaging aids their (and other students') content-area growth. Additionally, it sends a clear message to them that you care about them and recognize that their language is part of their identity.

Here are some ideas for encouraging translanguaging in a primarily English-speaking classroom:

- Let students brainstorm ideas of a new topic in their primary language.
- Use the closed-caption feature with other languages when showing a video (especially if there is one primary language group in the class).
- Encourage MLs to write an outline or rough draft of a writing assignment in their primary language before translating it into English.
- Invite MLs to write captions for images and artwork in English and another language.
- Provide links to multilingual glossaries.
- Directly teach cognates between English and your MLs' languages, if you know them.
- Let students research topics in their language on the internet and then translate back into English.
- Assign students of the same language groups to work together on occasion.
- Talk privately to students from the same language groups to see if they would be comfortable having a language buddy for the early weeks of arrival.

---

14 García, Ofelia, and Tatyana Kleyn, eds. *Translanguaging with multilingual students: Learning from classroom moments.* Routledge, 2016.

Technological Translations

I realize that coming up with contextual lessons for all content subjects takes a lot of time. Some schools are not structured in a way that provides content-area subject courses for MLs at the beginning levels of English proficiency. You can certainly provide some comprehensible input, but you can only scaffold so much for those at WIDA levels 1and 2, especially in secondary-level courses. This doesn't mean you ignore or give up, of course. Luckily, technology has come a long way in helping to provide tools for content-area translation so that MLs can get some content connected to the goals of the day.

Westernoff, et al.[15], provide a list of wonderful resources on how to use technology that support the implementation of other languages in the content classroom. These resources can provide tools for aligning with a translanguaging stance, even if you don't speak the languages of your MLs.

Here is a list:

- **Binogi Canada** [www.binogi.ca] is an online resource for supporting secondary students in learning mathematics and science concepts through content in their primary languages. They currently provide free online animated lessons in many languages, including Arabic, Dari, English, Finnish, French, German, Polish, Russian, Spanish, Somali, Swedish, Thai, Tigrinya, Turkish, and Ukrainian. Topics include the periodic table of elements, multiplication of decimals, food webs, and fractions. This viewing process allow MLs to first access the science in their primary language for initial conceptual understanding. With this base, they can better connect to the concepts of the class. They can also use closed captioning in whatever language might work for them.
- **Google** is probably the most common technological tool for educators. What might be new to you is that it provides a convenient tutorial called "Google Tools for English Language Learners" [www.techlearning.com/tl-advisor-blog/google-tools-for-english-language-learners]. Some highlights include being able to translate documents into other languages, though it's always good to have a proficient speaker look over it before you send it to parents. For quick in-class translations to help with content, it does the trick.
- Most are familiar with **Khan Academy** [www.khanacademy.org], but you may not know that they offer lessons in a variety of languages. The video lessons in all areas of the curriculum are accessible with subtitles.
- **Mentimeter** [www.mentimeter.com] is an online, interactive presentation tool accessible in three languages: English, Portuguese, and Spanish. It's also possible for students to contribute to a class-generated "word cloud" by providing words in their primary languages by typing on their Smart phone or iPad keyboards. Unlike with static PowerPoints, students can participate in polls, surveys, and short quizzes. When studying vocabulary, MLs can contribute and discuss words from various languages.
- **Scribjab** is an iPad app that allows MLs to read and create digital stories (text, illustrations, audio recordings) in multiple languages. ScribJab creates a space for children to

15 Westernoff, Fern, Stephaney Jones-Vo, and Paula Markus. *Powerful practices for supporting English learners: Elevating diverse assets and identities.* Corwin, 2021.

communicate about their stories and come to an enhanced appreciation of their own multilingual resources. The developers of this software are two education professors, Kelleen Toohey and Diane Daganais, who have worked with MLs for years. The originators of ScribJab are two Simon Fraser University professors (Kelleen Toohey and Diane Daganais) who have worked in language education for many years. ScribJab promotes reading and writing stories in all languages and allows students to word-process their books in a variety of languages. It also includes a drawing function so students can add their colorful artwork to the stories they write.

- **Vacaroo** [vocaroo.com] is a tool that can audio record and generate a matching QR code of the recording. How amazing is that! Students, teachers, parents, or other school personnel can record their voices and then upload them on QR codes that can be mounted on books, magazines, letters home, or other material. The best part is that the app can play back and record audio in any language so MLs can engage readily.

I believe that any technology is only as effective as the educator that implements it. Since interaction and integration is key for MLs' learning, I encourage these tools to be used in pairs and small groups or with the class as a whole, rather than putting MLs off to the side on a computer. Too often this is the solution teachers decide on when they don't have other more comprehensible and interactive strategies.

A helpful article on content literacy: [www.ascd.org/el/articles/disciplinary-literacy-a-shift-that-makes-sense]

4

CHAPTER FOUR

Collaboration for Content: Interaction is Essential

"If you want to go fast, go alone. If you want to go far, go together."

— AFRICAN PROVERB

The quote on the previous page speaks to the essence of collaboration. It does take longer to design lessons with lots of interaction, but your students will learn principles and key ideas with greater depth. The next issue is getting your students to talk to each other in meaningful ways.

"I put them in groups, but no one talks to each other," lamented one high school math teacher. "My students come from drastically different home situations. On top of that, there is a power dynamic that I don't know how to break."

This teacher acknowledged the challenges MLs often face in school environments dominated by White, English-speaking values, history, and education practices. Even though he wanted to create a community of respect, there was so much to overcome. MLs often bring identities from their home culture that are not recognized in school settings, especially when MLs are a low percentage of the school population. Building relationships with students begins with a conversation that recognizes the power at play. I had to create a system where MLs' opinions had meaning and added cultural capital, and as stated above, they brought these ideas to other classes and discussed those issues with their Latinx peers.

All learning is a sociocultural process, and this idea of social learning is imperative with MLs. Smaller, interactive spaces provide MLs with more opportunities to practice, apply, and learn the content language of the content area[1][2][3]. The best time to engage in small group or pair work is after you have introduced the overarching unit objectives, including language and content, and ideally essential questions.

How to Make Pair/Small Groups Work

I have heard teachers claim that "group work" doesn't work. I hear you. Examples of problems include only one student doing all the work, some students not engaging, or all physically moving in a group but not really talking. I too have seen these examples. Group or pair work needs structure and is more complex than first meets the eye. It takes time to structure group work interaction in a way that will result in learning.

DECIDE GROUPS AHEAD OF TIME

I am adamant that teachers should never say, "Get into groups and do _____." Form all groups intentionally ahead of time. If the exercise is short, you can have the students' number off or physically tell them who is in what group, but you should facilitate the formations. Far too often, I see worried or confused looks on students' faces, especially MLs, wondering if they should ask students to form a group or are concerned that no one will ask them to join. You can take away this anxiety by being the one to form the groups.

For MLs, it's essential to keep the following factors in mind.

---

1 Calderón, Margarita Espino, and Liliana Minaya-Rowe. Preventing long-term ELs: *Transforming schools to meet core standards*. Corwin Press, 2010.

2 Coles-Ritchie, Marilee. *Inciting change in secondary English language programs: The case of Cherry High School*. Springer, 2009.

3 Haynes, Judie, and Debbie Zacarian. *Teaching English language learners across the content areas*. ASCD, 2010.

1. Think about the MLs' level of English proficiency. If an ML is at the beginning or intermediate stages of fluency, they are less likely to contribute if they are the only one at that stage in the group. Many MLs, understandably, are afraid to make errors in front of their peers. One way to help mitigate the stress is to place at least two MLs in each group, preferably with a bilingual student who speaks their language. Teachers sometimes tend to distribute the few MLs they might have in a content class in each group, which can feel isolating. In addition, it might be hard for them to keep up with the group conversation if they are the only ones in the process of learning English.

2. Consider other factors students might have in relation to your content area, such as background knowledge, cultural knowledge, lived experiences, personality, willingness to make mistakes or reach out to others, and how long they've been in the United States.

3. Group roles can create an atmosphere of cooperation and learning. It's important to assign MLs a role in which they can stretch and is consistent with their linguistic abilities, so they don't get too frustrated. For example, a student at the beginning stages of development might have the role of illustrating the project or being the timekeeper. Those in more advanced stages could have the roles of connector or reporter. The types and names of roles within groups are numerous. Here are a few: facilitator, project manager, timekeeper, notetaker, resource manager, process observer, summarizer, questioner, connector, and participation tracker. It's important that the roles reflect the project and that they are inherently beneficial for the group's tasks.

4. Within the groups, students should be allowed to use their primary language (one they are most comfortable using in that content area). I would discuss with students how to use their primary language within the group in a way that is respectful for all involved. For example, let's say you have a group with four students. Two of the students speak Spanish (one is at a WIDA level 1 and the other at a WIDA level 3 in English). The other two students are monolingual. It's important to explicitly state that sometimes the two Spanish-speaking students might need to speak in Spanish for clarity. Still, the Level 3–speaking student will briefly share what they discussed with the English-speaking students. The English-speaking students need to understand that when the other two speak Spanish, it is not to talk about them or leave them out; it's to make sure they understand and can contribute to the project. All students can be explicitly taught how to use the comprehensible input strategies discussed in the previous chapter.

Fishbowl Activity: Make Explicit What is Hidden

Group work is enhanced when you explicitly describe the hidden expectations of what will happen in pairs or group work. I recommend the following ideas to help all students understand the group work process. Group work is more productive when each student has a role. I assign those roles and always create the groups ahead of time, based on several factors I will explain below.

Make sure to model group work. Ask a few students (ideally ahead of time) to sit in a circle in the middle of the classroom as if they are in a small group. All the rest of the students in the class stand in a circle around them. Give these students the role of jotting down aspects of cooperative group behavior.

Fishbowl

- Preselected students will model a group activity.
- Everyone shares their names.
- Each person shares the role they have been given. The group briefly goes over the action of this role.
- The students begin working on the task. I assign a short task for this fishbowl activity, so students are not standing too long.
- After they finish the task, one student presents the result of the task.
- Ask the students in the outside circle to share what went well with the group work, then ask if there is anything the students could do to make the group work even more smoothly. Write their specific ideas on the board or projector.
- Instruct all the students to return to their desks and write at least three ideas they can do in the future to contribute to positive group work.
- Another idea is to have all the teachers on your team do a video about what an effective group discussion looks like and what a poor discussion looks like. The teachers act out their roles. Students get a kick out of seeing their teachers in student roles.

Group work flourishes when all students buy into the process and the product. Assessing group work has additional aspects to consider, especially in mixed linguistic and ability grouping. With every task within a group work assignment, both process- and product-related skills should be assessed. Group contributions must be translated into individual grades, raising fairness and equity issues.

The process is enhanced when students have time to assess their contributions and focus on what others in the group did well, rather than having students state what others could have done better. Many process skills could be included, such as (a) respectfully listening to classmates even when they have opposing views, (b) managing conflict around differences in ideas or approaches, (c) keeping the group on track both during and between meetings, (d) inviting quiet students in the group to share, (e) inviting talkative students to step back from sharing and give others a turn.

Another tip is to have students individually jot down some ideas they want to discuss before they get in their groups. If their ideas are already outlined and fresh, they can get right down to discussing.

After the group has worked together, assess how much each student learned. Independent reflections, journal entries, short quizzes, or ticket-out-the-door slips can accomplish this. On the next page is an example of a template for student self-evaluation during group work:

Self-Evaluation for Group Work

	Always*	Sometimes	Not at all
Participated actively through my role			
Listened actively to my classmates			
Encouraged my classmates			
Paid attention to stepping in and stepping back			

Describe what went well in your group (more than one language used, cultural background shared, creative responses, follow-up questions to take the conversation deeper, etc.)

1.

2.

3.

Describe what you or others could have done better.

1.

2.

3.

* *Honest self-reflection is more important than answering "always" to each of the questions.*

It's important that the students know ahead of time that they will be completing a self-evaluation and what components are on it. This can help them contribute and encourage others to stay on task. The expectations are clear.

I suggest changing and adding to the self-evaluation with specifics to the task the students are completing. To encourage translanguaging and cultural contributions, you can add specific questions or hints showing how you think group work is enhanced when students share ideas specific to their cultural and linguistic heritage.

Dialogue Journals

Dialogue journals involve more than one person writing ideas in the same notebook or journal. For example, a student writes an idea on a topic and then asks a question. The respondent, usually the teacher, answers the questions and writes a question back again. They are often used in language arts classes but could also benefit MLs in all content area classes.

When I taught ninth-grade language arts on the Mexican-U.S. border, I used dialogue journals to connect individually with my students and assess their writing ability. Topics could include what they knew and thought about the content we were studying, what they were doing socially, and what they wanted to share about their family and community. The questions I asked were open-ended. I encouraged them to write the answers and also to ask me questions.

You might ask: How could you do that with 200+ students?

1. I had five classes. I had first period students turn theirs in on Monday, second period on Tuesday, etc.
2. Students wrote in the journal for about five to ten minutes each day, but I wrote back to them just once a week.
3. I didn't grade them—I just read them and wrote comments and questions back to them.

I looked forward to this assignment. I enjoyed learning from each student as it helped me connect personally. In addition, I learned more about what they knew and what I needed to scaffold for them in writing and other content.

Question Stem Signal Share Assess (QSSSA)

This is a strategy that can be used throughout your lessons. It works especially well if the content requires you to teach from a "direct instruction" method, as you are teaching a new concept but want to keep all your students engaged. For MLs, this strategy gives them time to process, possibly look up words in a dictionary, and consult with a peer before they are asked to share in front of the entire class. It's effective in any content area.

- **Question**: Ask students an open-ended question to connect to the concept you are going to teach. Make sure you write it on the board or have it projected so MLs can hear it and see it.

  — How can algebra solve real-world problems?
  — How can history be true if it is written by humans who are fallible?

- **Stem or sentence frame**: Next provide a stem, such as "I am not sure what this is about, but I think it might be . . .," or a sentence frame: "I think it could solve _____ if it ______" to provide a scaffold for their answer. Require the students to write down their answer on white boards, graphic organizers, content notebooks, or scratch paper.
- **Signal**: Give students a set amount of time to work independently. Put a timer up on the projector or use your watch/phone. Tell them to let you know they are done by turning their paper over or raising their hands.
- **Share**: Group students in pairs or threes to share their responses. This short activity usually works best if students are grouped with those sitting near them. Make sure you indicate clearly who is in each group. Be aware of MLs' language abilities and possible bilingual mentors as you develop seating charts.
- **Assess**: Walk around the room, listening to the student's answers. Invite them to share their answers with the whole class. For MLs, I usually quietly ask while they are working in their partners or small groups if they would be willing to share with the class. Allow them to share in whatever language is more comfortable for them if you can translate or have a student translate.

Experiments/Collaboration in Groups

It's important to place MLs in a group that understands how to make what they say comprehensible (e.g., using a computer translation program) or that there is a bilingual partner they can speak with. As they move through the steps of the experiment, MLs practice reading comprehension as they read the directions, listen to understand the steps, write the results, and describe what they did. Many secondary teachers and college professors in STEAM (Science, Technology, Engineering, Arts, and Math) assign their students certain roles for classroom experiments. They have observed that some students can cooperatively troubleshoot, share observations, and practice communication. Adding "roles" to experiments can bring additional value to group learning in terms of linguistic accessibility and inclusion.

I explained a bit about roles in the section on grouping students. Here are specific roles for experiments:

- **Project Manager**: Students in this role provide the group with the instructions and help with time management, ensuring that students work efficiently, stay on task, and meet all required steps of the project or experiment. This role builds skills in communication, organization, leadership, and time management. This role is not constrained by motor skills or tactile sensory sensitivities and can be adapted to accommodate MLs who are deaf, hard of hearing, or have visual impairments. Each group usually has just one project manager.
- **Technician**: Students in this role are the main "hands" for the activity and do most of the building, mixing, or other tactile work (based on directions from the project manager). This role builds motor skills, direction-following skills, and attention to detail. This role is not constrained by English proficiency and can be adapted to accommodate students who are differently abled. Groups of more than four students might have more than one technician.

- **Data Analyst**: Students in this role record and analyze the data generated by the group. This role builds reasoning skills, organization skills, and numerical literacy. This role can be adapted for MLs of different levels of fluency by translating language-heavy directions. An ML who has mathematical knowledge and is at a lower proficiency level can succeed in this role. Groups of more than four students might have more than one data analyst.
- **Reporter**: Students in this role communicate the group's findings or present the group's design to the class. In this role, students summarize results, determine how to best share a project, and create presentation materials (e.g., slides, poster, etc.). This role builds communication and presentation skills and can be adapted through using a translation tool, making sure all students use visuals and gestures to explain their results. Groups of more than four students might have more than one reporter.

Total Physical Response

Psychologist Dr. James Asher developed a method of teaching vocabulary called "Total Physical Response" (TPR), based on the experience of how children learn their first language. When children learn their home language, their parents or caregivers are usually physically involved in using language. They demonstrate and instruct, and the child responds in kind. No one demands or requires a baby or toddler to speak at all, only to listen and understand—which is to say, to comprehend. Young children usually observe and listen to know what to do. In essence, TPR creates a neural link between speech and action.

TPR is not used as much with adolescent learners as it is with children, but it has a lot of benefits for MLs in content-area classrooms. I would suggest using it occasionally or for short time periods. Here's why:

- Movement paired with language connects neural pathways for learning
- Left and right sides of their brains are activated
- Listening skills are enhanced
- Only receptive language is used so MLs can participate with a lower affective filter
- Secondary students will appreciate the movement and potential for humor
- Learners who prefer kinesthetic and visual activities will engage
- Learners are participating as a group so individual learners are not singled out
- It's simple for teachers to prepare

When to use it:

- Vocabulary, particularly verbs
- Difficult-to-explain actions (think wiggle, slide, launch)
- Storytelling and narrative language
- Imperatives and classroom language

HOW TO USE TPR IN CLASS

Below is a basic method for using Total Physical Response in the classroom:

- The teacher (or another student) performs an action, both demonstrating and saying it (e.g., "This is a vertical line"). Be prepared to exaggerate, use gesture, facial expressions, and props if necessary.
- Call on all students to stand up and repeat the action.
- Repeat once more.
- Write the word or phrase on the board.
- Repeat with other words or phrases.

TPR geometry example:

Following is an example from a secondary math teacher named Kristin Kamenar:

> As I started to think about how I could use this type of activity in my math classroom I immediately thought of the basic vocabulary that I need to teach my geometry students at the beginning of the year. I came up with a series of movements that would help my students better understand basic geometric terms and labeling conventions. I created actions to go along with terms such as Point, Line, Plane, Collinear Points, Ray, different ways to classify angles, as well as a few others. You can check out some of the symbols in my TPR presentation (docs.google.com/presentation/d/1mLXG6nTk7AvYxaXUIwRKIt2qIG4q12Hck-RHKo687qzU/edit#slide=id.p) that I have posted online: In the past, students have struggled with naming conventions that pertain to basic geometric vocabulary. By using a total physical response activity, students will have a physical reminder that will help them with naming and labeling conventions.

Found Poems

Is poetry only for English class? Think again. Engaging in "found poetry" can provide a level playing field in almost any subject matter. One definition of *found poems* is that the poem is created using only words, phrases, or quotations that have been selected and rearranged from another text. The text can be an academic article, newspaper, textbook, or novel from your content area. Students create found poems by choosing phrases from the original text that is particularly meaningful or interesting to them. They then organize the phrases or words around a theme or message. Writing found poems is a structured way to have students review material and synthesize their learning.

Ideas for implementation:

1. **Students create a list of words, phrases, and quotations.**
   Individually, students review a text related to a unit of study in a content area. The texts could be in English or the ML's primary languages. Give students highlighters so they can highlight words, phrases, or quotations that are particularly interesting or meaningful as they review the texts. It's useful for students to identify at least fifteen words or phrases within the text, so they have plenty of ideas to choose from as they

compose their poems. Depending on the language acquisition level of the student, you could provide shorter passages.

2. **Students decide on a theme based on the content.**
   In intentionally mixed language groups, students decide on a theme or message connected to their study content. Of course, there are a lot of different options; depending on your goals, you can limit or expand the choices. It might be helpful to suggest brainstorming many ideas in a short, timed period. Tell them that there are no wrong ideas for this free-form list. That way, they have a variety of ideas to choose from.

Secondary science teacher Rachel David shares how she created "found poems" in her classroom:

> This is where it will get a bit tricky—scientific papers don't have beautiful language; in fact, they are full or technical, jargony words that you would normally adapt or translate in a piece of science communication (case in point in my paper, abdomen and gastrointestinal tract vs. belly or tummy). But, sorry, this isn't allowed here! You must work with the words in front of you, so you must be creative and see the potential in those more challenging words (including any double-meaning or colloquial uses). It might help to have an idea of what you want the poem to be about, its key message, and whether you follow the same kind of structure as the paper.

She said she wanted to tell the story of the vagus nerve and its fascinating role as part of the gut-brain axis as the theme of her paper. To keep it short and straightforward, she used some of the technical language in the paper but ended it with a bonus word—"'wanderer"—to make it more human.

wanderer nerve (the vagus nerve)

It's a complex relationship
the gut and the brain
A long path
from brainstem to bowel
A vast array of
emotions, cognitive and intestinal functions
And one nerve
connecting gut and brain
controlling mood and emotions
influencing stress, anxiety, depression
'Wanderer' nerve
signals butterfliues in my abdomen

By Rachel David

Source: Breit, S. et al (2018) Vagus nerve as modulator of the brain-gut axis in psychiatric and inflammatory disorders. *Front. Psychiatry.* doi.org/10.3389/fpsyt.2018.00044

3. **Students select an additional language.**
Found poems only use words that have been collected from a previously written source. So, once students have selected a theme and a message, they may need to review their materials again to collect additional language. This process encourages deep-level thinking and the process of connecting ideas. Encourage MLs to use translators and draw on their linguistic repertoires.

4. **Students compose a poem.**
To make it easier to arrange, I suggest that students cut out the phrases they want to use or write all the words and phrases on slips of paper. That way, they can move the slips around until the poem is to their liking. They can't add their own words when creating a found poem, but they can repeat words or phrases as often as they like. Also, when putting together found poems, they don't need to use all the words or phrases they have previously selected.

5. **Share Poems**
It can be motivating when students have the opportunity to share or publish their work. Writing for an audience can add to their creativity and attention to the poem. There are lots of ideas for sharing their work:

- Each group can read their poem like reader's theater, where some students read lines together and others read alone.
- Poems can be pinned on a bulletin board.
- Each group can pass their poems to the next group and ask for feedback or clarification. As a group, they write a comment and then pass the poem again to the left for another comment. Depending on how much time you have, you might allow for three or four passes, or you might have time for students to comment on all their classmates' poems.

Discuss

End the "found poem" lesson with a final discussion highlighting what the poems reveal about the content or goals of this section. Following are some possible prompts:

- What are common themes in all these poems?
- How are they different?
- What surprised you when reading them?
- What did you learn about ______________ by writing and reading the poems?

CHAPTER FIVE

Choice in Assessment

5

"Classroom assessment can stimulate multilingual learner engagement and represent the interplay between content and language as a means of advancing student learning."

— MARGO GOTTLIEB

One of the most equitable and encouraging ways to connect MLs to your content area classroom is to allow choice. Choice does not "dumb down" the content, rather it allows space for MLs to show, tell, write what they know. It helps change the phrase language barrier to language opportunity that builds on their own learning and lift of the learning of others. Thoughtfully planning choice within assessments is key for students to build on their capabilities and their autonomy. It should be aligned with their strengths, the content and language objectives and the standards of the content area unit studied.

This graphic demonstrates pretend choice:

Image:
Dr. Tim Clark
byotnetwork.com/2016/01/19/choice-for-personalized-learning

While choice is key for equitable assessment, it can be overwhelming if the acceptable choices are too numerous or not explained clearly. Scaffolding the process of assessment choice is helpful. I appreciate the guidelines shared by Snyder & Fenner in their book *Culturally Responsive Teaching for Multilingual Learners*. They suggest you organize choice in terms of **who** students wish to work with; **what** academic tasks they do to demonstrate learning; and **where** do their work.

WHO

Provide opportunities for students to try how what it feels like to work independently, in pairs or in teacher constructed small groups. Ask students to think about which they prefer and why. Share that there isn't one way of working that is better than another. Allow students to choose one way of doing the assignment.

WHAT

As you decide on the content that you would like to assess, consider how to build choice into that task. I would suggest only giving 2-3 options as a start. These options should offer opportunities to demonstrate progress towards the language and content standards. You can structure the tasks so there are differing levels of scaffolding. For example, here's a way to offer different assessment in a secondary math class studying linear functions.

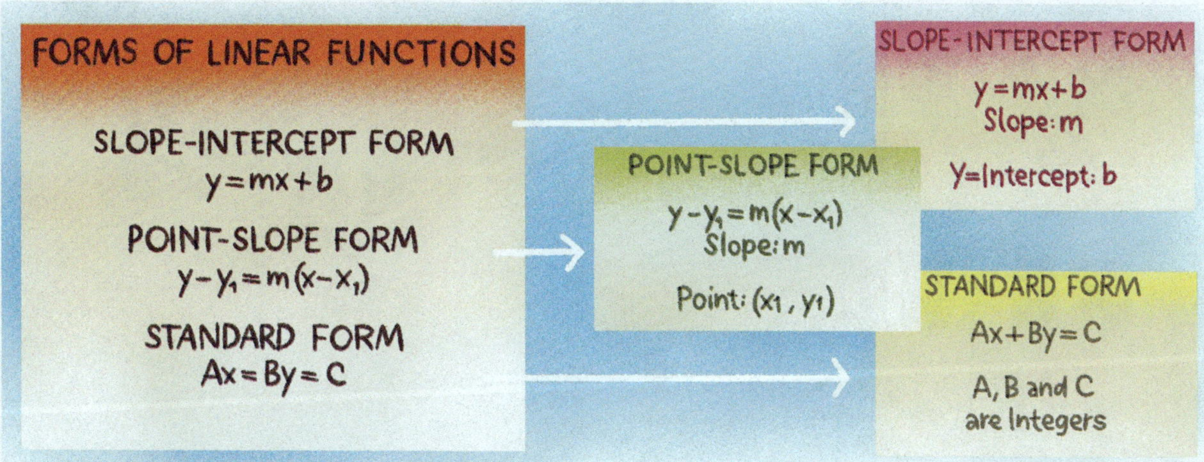

Option #1: In pairs or small groups, students can create an infographic on the computer.

Option #2: Individually, a student creates a brief PowerPoint/keynote describing the forms of linear functions. Bonus points for sharing terms in another language.

Option #3: In pairs, create a chart drawing free form, the forms of linear functions.

Here's another example for a science class where students are learning new vocabulary words on climate change. Provide a list of no more that 12 new words.

Option #1: In small groups, create a concept map with words grouped together that are related.

Option #2: In pairs, develop flash cards with the new words. On one side, student writes their own definition, on the other side they write the word and a picture.

WHERE

Offering MLs options about where they do their work can be another way of providing a welcoming space. In your classroom, you can set up places where students can work alone, in small groups, or in pairs. It would also be useful to have a carpet where they can sit on the floor, and a place where they can stand. In a vibrant classroom I visited, the teacher put cut open tennis balls on the bottom of the chairs to allow for easy movement of the chairs without making sounds.

Traditional classroom layouts, with rows of tables all facing the same direction, don't facilitate communication between students. Consider smaller, circular clusters that dissolve hierarchy and enable dialog.

Underlying Assessment of MLs

The more you can involve MLs in their own learning, the more invested they will be. At the beginning of the year or after they take their state mandated assessment for placement, invite each student to review their scores and have them set goals for their language development. Concentrate on the area of the assessment that focuses on content area learning or academic learning. The designated ELD (English Language Development) Coordinator can help explain this section to you if you are not familiar. WIDA is the most commonly used assessment tool. You can ask the coordinator or administrator for the Access for ELLs assessment. From there, you can look at the ACCESS score reports and Can Do Descriptors for their grade level. At this point, you have a better idea of what students Can Do at their language development level. When students know you have invested time into seeing what their strengths are and what they need to work on, they are more likely to view you as a partner in their education path.

Self-Assessment

I cannot over-stress the importance of self-assessment for the growth of MLs. I have heard often that MLs get frustrated because they cannot see the progress they are making in language. Assessments are often not systemic and teachers do not always explain through feedback where they are in relation to the goals of the class. Self-assessment can guide MLs towards meaning making in a content area. It intrinsically connects what they are learning to their passions, communities, cultures, and identities as they reflect on formative and summative assessment data see what they know and in what areas they struggle. Self-assessment can give you insights into their perceptions and understandings about a variety of educational tasks. These insights in combination with data, create a comprehensive picture of MLs' progress. One of the premier scholars in ML assessment is Margo Gottlieb[1]. She shares a variety of ways that MLs can be involved in assessing their learning.

Mark the following as accurately as you can:	I can	I think I can	I can't
1. Explain what hypothesis means			
2. Name the genus and species of common animals as cats and dogs			
3. Read a mercury thermometer			
4. Identify at least 10 internal body parts			
5. Use a microscope to examine data up close			
6. State reasonable, testable hypotheses and explain what makes them so			

Gottlieb suggests starting with standard-referenced criteria or exemplars. Look at the standards for your content area to create a checklist for your students. For beginning MLs, it's helpful to translate the checklist into their primary language or to give them time to translate it. Make the checklist simple. Here's an example:

Another idea is the tic-tac-toe assessment as a cumulating task that can be used to assess student's understanding of the content. They are encouraged to move through three different tasks in a certain amount of time so that you extend from their strengths to developing areas that are less developed.

A tic-tac-toe grid is a way to add choice for students while providing essential information about their growth for you as the teacher. You can structure tasks in the grid that specifically shows students' comprehension, analysis, and/or application of any given standard. Here's how it works:

1 Gottlieb, Margo. *Assessing English language learners: Bridges to educational equity: Connecting academic language proficiency to student achievement*. Corwin Press, 2016.

- Students are given a 3 x 3 grid just like tic-tac-toe board.
- In each box, you write and activity or task for the students to accomplish. Options include:

  - 9 activities related to the content that you are covering
  - 8 activities, leaving the middle blank for a "free choice"
  - Activities accessible to all levels of language proficiencies
  - Activities based on a variety of learning preferences (kinesthetic, visusal, auditor)
  - Activities using paper and pencil or technology to complete
  - Activities that can be done solo, with pairs, or in small groups

Encourage students choose one activity per column, row or diagonal with a total of three. Mix up the activities in a way that the students have a variety of experiences at the end.

Choice in writing and assessment can be motivating and builds in differentiation, so you don't have to create a bunch of assignments for each student to meet them where they are. One of the most versatile and creative writing strategies is the RAFT (Role, Audience, Format, Topic). As the teacher, you can provide parameters for this assignment connected to a goal or standard from your content area. This assignment/assessment leads students to understand the purpose for writing, the audience they are writing to, the varied formats of writing in everyday life, and the specific topic that will be their theme. It's fantastic for Multilingual Learners because they can delve deep into a topic without providing a language-heavy document. All students benefit from higher-order thinking, creatively stretching and focusing directly on how they need to write to address specific audiences.

The following questions help students define with more depth the different aspects of the RAFT paper.

Role of the Writer: Who or what are you as the writer? An activist? A soldier? The President?

Audience: To whom are you writing? A friend? Your teacher? Readers of a newspaper?

Format: In what format are you writing? A letter? A poem? A speech?

Topic and strong verb: What are you writing about? Why? What's the subject or the point?

Ways to teach RAFT explicitly, especially the first time you introduce it.

1. Project a completed RAFT example.
2. Describe each of the components of the RAFT: role, audience, format, and topic. (It may be helpful to have students in small groups create a large chart paper or a bulletin board for future reference).
3. On a projector, model how to write responses to the prompts and discuss the key elements as a class. Keep this as simple and concise as possible for newcomers to the language.
4. Have students practice responding to prompts individually or in small groups. At first,

CIVIL RIGHTS

JOHN LEWIS	US-CITIZENS	POSTER	*Equal Rights*
ARTIST	CONGRESS	LETTER	*Segregation*
BLACK TEACHER	BUSINESS LEADERS	SPEECH	*Little Rock Nine*
PRES. JOHNSON	COLLEGE STUDENTS	POEM	*Jim Crow*

it may be best to have all students react to the same prompt so the class can learn from varied responses.

The RAFT strategy has been adapted for students from K–12 and beyond. I use RAFT in my college classroom. Thinking of these four different aspects pushes them to think more deeply. I have listed some strategies that are particularly useful for MLs.

- MLs can review the RAFT concept and assignment orally first. Have students work in pairs to explain what is meant by role, audience, format, and topic.
- In small groups, students can create anchor charts describing and illustrating each of the elements of RAFT.
- Have students role-play explanations of the different aspects of RAFT assignment.
- Allow students to create bi- or multi-lingual responses to the RAFT assignment.
- Encourage less language-heavy formats such as brochures, slides, or posters for those at the beginning stages of proficiency.

- Pair students together to create RAFT assignments with clear expectations for both students. Be mindful of the linguistic capabilities of both students for the final product.
- Provide models of RAFTs for students to use as scaffolding for completing their own.
- MLs who know the content or topic of the RAFT may be able to produce more depth within the RAFT, especially if they are encouraged to look up material in their primary language.

Sample RAFT for a math class:

Role	Audience	Format	Topic
Exponent	Jury of law	Instructions	Laws of exponents
Percent	Young child	How-to guide	Ways to calculate percentage
Parts of a graphs (multiple roles)	YouTube	Script	Graphing principles
Container (gallon, bucket, etc.)	Self	Dear Diary	Volume Measurements

Formulaic Expressions

MLs often have a lot more to say than their level of English language proficiency will allow. As mentioned earlier language production (speaking, writing) usually come later than language reception (listening, reading). As such sentence frames or starters can provide understanding in the pre-production and early production stages of language proficiency by providing vocabulary and structure isn't easy to access on their own. Sentence frames are particularly helpful when writing about more linguistically complex ideas common in content area subjects including:

- Analysis/Prediction
- Explanation
- Cause and Effect

Sentence frames or starters guide MLs to understand key ideas for analysis within a text so they can complete a writing or discussion activity. They are scaffolds for building that can assist them to analyze and write about content without the use of the frames as they develop their proficiency. It's useful to differentiate sentence frames—offering some straightforward phrases that prompt the use of specific vocabulary for early MLs, and offering other frames that are either more open-ended (thus reducing the level of scaffold) or prompting the students to make more complex connections to other concepts. It is important that you not overuse sentence frames. Making the use of sentence frames mandatory for all students or using them too frequently can take away from students' creativity and lead to parroting of phrases rather than deeper thought. Once students are able to produce structured responses on their own, sentence frames can be eliminated. Students should understand how the sentences constructed through use of frames and starters are used to convey meaning, and eventually contribute to larger written work such as paragraphs and essays. Here are some examples:

ANALYSIS

- I anticipate that ______ causes ______.
- I think that will happen because ______.
- I think ________ might ________ because I know that ______.
- If ________ then ________
- Based on the experiment, I can infer that the ____ will increase and the ____ will decrease.

EXPLANATION

- One reason ______ might happen is because ______.
- Another reason ______ might happen is because ______.
- At first, I thought ______ but now, I think ______ because ______
- I like how the author uses ______ to show ______.
- I like/don't like ______ because ______.
- My opinion is ______ because ______.
- The most important message is ______ because ______.
- The ____ has ___ sides/angles.
- I can solve this problem in the following ways ______, ______, and ______.

CAUSE AND EFFECT

- ______ is the most likely cause for ______.
- When happened ______ then ______ to place as a result.
- I think was caused by because ______.
- The effects of were ______.
- The reason for was ______.
- ______ occurred, and consequently ______.
- That wasn't caused by ______ because ______.

SCIENTIFIC LANGUAGE FUNCTIONS SENTENCE STRUCTURE FRAMES

Sequence

We saw that first, _________, then, ________, and at the end, _________.

Hypothesize

If _________ had________, then______would have ____________.

Identify relationships

This _______is necessary for ________ because it __________. Compare This _________ is similar to that ______because both ____________.

Contrast

This ____________ is different from that ________ because one has ________ and the other doesn't have ________.

Estimate

Looking at the _________________, I think there are______________.

Disagree

I don't think the evidence supports ________because_______.

I don't agree with that statement because __________________________.

Table adapted from californiascienceproject.ucr.edu

Demonstrations

Before students try experiments, teachers often demonstrate the experiment first. This can help the students see the entire process before delving in and ensure that all students are aware of safety procedures. So that MLs can follow along also, I would suggest that each item used in the demonstration is labeled with a card taped to it or nearby. Also, project the directions that you are saying so all can see as well as hear you. Pause often and ask students to think/pair questions to connect them to the process and to allow time for needed clarification or translation with a partner. Most MLs won't feel comfortable interrupting the class.

Presentations

Presentations are a wonderful way for MLs to express what they have learned about a certain topic, because sharing involves comprehensible input through visuals and gestures. They can work on pronunciation and clarity and share ideas that might be difficult to write out. Presentations are a common practice in almost every occupation, and they are often done in collaboration with their colleagues. In addition, research confirms that MLs can acquire English more readily through oral language practice within meaningful academic activities. The process of organizing and delivering content through a presentation can encourage deep thinking.

Nonetheless, speaking in front of others can be scary, especially for adolescent students who are trying to impress their peers. For MLs, their anxiety can be heightened as they are trying to communicate in a language they are still in the process of learning. Below are some ideas that can help alleviate affective filter by structuring presentation in the secondary classroom:

TRANSLANGUAGING SUPPORT

It is essential to provide support for MLs, especially at the beginning level of proficiency. They should be allowed to research and discuss the topics of the presentation in their primary language before they figure out what they want to present in English. They also might need a bit of time before they are comfortable presenting, especially if they have been in the country less than six months. Think about what vocabulary, language features, organizational structures, and peers they may need to feel secure in the process. It's important that they have the opportunity to present with a small group or partner before they are expected to present alone. You can provide students with speaking frames, graphic organizers, and notecards. Let students know that you want everyone to participate, but not everyone needs to speak the same amount of time.

TOPIC CHOICE

Because of the extra effort to give presentations, you can scaffold the process of presentations by allowing MLs to choose the subtopic with your unit goals. MLs can rely on some of their background knowledge and they will be more motivated to dig into the research. It's useful to create a curated list for them to choose from so they don't flounder too much. By keeping the presentations within a topic, MLs can apply new vocabulary, demonstrate their learning, and feel more confident in their knowledge. When students are presenting information on a topic they have researched, we remind them to summarize using their own words and to give credit when using someone else's words.

LENGTH—LESS IS MORE

It's more likely that all students in the class will benefit when the presentations are shorter rather than longer. I would suggest presentations that are between three to five minutes. Shorter, more frequent presentations can help MLs practice their presentations skill with smaller, less overwhelming tasks. As they get more comfortable, they can do longer presentations at the end of a unit or semester with a group or partner for seven to ten minutes.

SPICE IT UP!

To create some variation in presentations, it's important to have students work in a variety of different groups. You can combine students based on a variety of factors and make sure that they are all getting to work with different classmates. Sometimes the presentations can be pairs and sometimes small groups (preferably three to five). If the presentations are short, students can work in small groups but present their subtopic individually. Another way to create variety is to have them present with posters, slide presentations on the projector, photovoice, demonstrations, or on the document camera.

AUDIENCE ENGAGEMENT

We all know that students will space out during presentations if they are not asked to engage in specific ways. I always have a task for their peers to do while they are presenting. It's so much more motivating to present to a room that is actually listening to you and showing respect. It's also a great way to teach everyone listening skills. Ask the students to fill out a graphic organizer, write down new ideas they've learned, ask questions, or complete a short evaluation.

Presenter & Topic	Two things I learned	Presentation skills they did well

TECHNOLOGY SUPPORT

MLs come to the secondary classroom from all kinds of backgrounds. They may come from a school with lots of technology, but more likely they will have had less experience using technology than what most schools in North America provide. Some MLs come from difficult circumstances of interrupted schooling or lack of resources. Thus, starting small and simple is best. Pairing MLs with students who have some understanding of how to use technology is helpful, as are demonstrations. You might need to break up the classroom into mini-groups so you and other students can do some tech training. Seeing what you expect from a sample...

TEACHER FEEDBACK

Think of student presentations as a process rather than a product, especially with MLs. If the focus is on the practice of confidence and skills they are gaining, rather than the score, their affective filter will be lowered. At the same time, you want them to put in an effort and try their best. Providing a simple rubric for them to follow beforehand is useful. It can guide their work and provide clarity for expectations.

SAMPLE Presentation Rubric

Category	Scoring Criteria	Total Points	Score
Organization 15 points	The type of presentation is appropriate for the topic and audience.	5	
	Information is presented in a logical sequence.	5	
	Presentation appropriately cites requisite number of references.	5	
Content 45 points	Introduction is attention-getting, lays out the problem well, and establishes a framework for the rest of the presentation.	5	
	Technical terms are well-defined in language appropriate for the target audience.	5	
	Presentation contains accurate information.	10	
	Material included is relevant to the overall message/purpose.	10	
	Appropriate amount of material is prepared, and points made reflect their relative importance.	10	
	There is an obvious conclusion summarizing the presentation.	5	
Presentation 40 points	Speaker maintains good eye contact with the audience and is appropriately animated (e.g., gestures, moving around, etc.).	5	
	Speaker uses a clear, audible voice.	5	
	Delivery is poised, controlled, and smooth.	5	
	Uses clear, grammatically correct language.	5	
	Visual aids are well prepared, informative, effective, and not distracting.	5	
	Length of presentation is within the assigned time limits.	5	
	Information was well communicated.	10	
	Total Points	100	

Short Translanguaging Writing Assessment

Sometimes you want your students to answer a prompt so you can quickly assess how well they have understood a certain concept. Though translating tools are helpful, they can slow MLs down. This technique allow them to write in their primary language without using a translation device.

- **Prompt**: Provide all the students with a writing prompt. Let them know the expectations, such as they need to have at least three ideas or it needs to be at least five sentences. Make sure the prompt is projected or written on the board.
- **Write**: Within a time frame, allow all students to write the response in their primary language.
- **Known words**: For MLs, have them reread their response and highlight all the words they wrote in their language that they also know in English. These might be high frequency words like "the," "and," or "that."
- **Cognates**: After they identify known words, have them look for cognates, such as "chocolate" (English) and "chocolate" (Spanish).
- **Bilingual or ELL Dictionary**: The final step is for them to look up all the remaining words in their dictionary.

By using this strategy, MLs are able to get their ideas about the content out first and then work on creating the writing prompt in English. It helps with fluency of ideas.

Self-Assessment

One of the most powerful tools you have is assigning self-assessments, which give you a window into a student's understanding of the topic and sometimes a more accurate view of what they know and don't know. Self-reflection can provide motivation and help students be more aware of specific elements they need to work on.

For students to self-assess in a way that's useful for their growth, they need to have a model. For example, share a sample presentation that you recorded previously. Each student would have a copy of the rubric that is being used.

T: The rubric says that you need to speak clearly. Did all the members speak clearly? Just because a student is speaking in an accent different from yours does not mean they are not speaking clearly.

T: In pairs, I want you to discuss how you might evaluate them on the rubric.

Give the students a few minutes to discuss.

T: Carla and Alim, what did you discuss?

Carla: Alim and I thought that the students were clear but quiet.

T: OK, so the rubric says, "Student speaks clearly all the time, volume is appropriate, stays on topic 100 percent of the time, and uses vocabulary that is appropriate for the audience."

Alim: I would say they did well on all but the volume.

T: So, the rubric says that 4 is the highest and 1 is the lowest. How might you evaluate yourself?

Carla: I would give myself a 3 and say that I need to work on speaking louder.

T: I appreciate how you've evaluated yourself with specific feedback. That will help you know how to improve in the future.

By modeling self-assessment in this way, you are helping students understand how to read the rubric and think about giving themselves specific feedback, and in turn they can see their growth and where they need to improve.

Self-assessment helps students feel more engaged in the learning process. They develop insights about their own language process and are accountable for their learning. They also gain confidence about their abilities, enhance their capacity to see and make corrections, and create specific goals to increase their language learning.

Peer Assessment

If you're asking peers to evaluate each other, it's important to give them a lot of practice and guidance. You don't want to have students complaining that so-and-so evaluated them harshly or gave them a bad score because they "don't like them." I prefer to ask peers to evaluate what their peers added to the presentation and not what they can improve.

Peer and Self-Evaluation: Math Expert's Presentation

Student's Name	Role	**Contributions to the presentation** completed all aspects of their role, cheered us on, stayed on task, had creative ideas, provided translation, etc.
	Scribe/Recorder	
	Presenter/Timekeeper	
	Equalizer (makes sure all members contribute/stay on task)	

CHAPTER SIX

6

Tokenism and Trauma-Informed Practice

"We can transform collective trauma into collective healing by creating spaces for people to come together and share their experiences and by providing opportunities for healing practices and cultural revitalization"

— EDUARDO DURAN

My intent with this book was to create a usable guide for secondary teachers of MLs. Of course, within each section there could be numerous subsections that could focus more specifically on intersectionality of MLs in regards to race, gender, sexual orientation, class, status, and ability. Providing the support necessary for each group is beyond the scope of this book, but I encourage you to find resources for those specific needs. Within these categories are two issues that are likely to arise in your classrooms when working with MLs: tokenism and trauma.

Tokenism

As teachers who recognize the gifts MLs bring to the classroom, you could have a tendency to call on them to provide insights within a class discussion that connects with their language or culture. Tension arises with allowing space for them to share—in other words, "tokenizing" them. Tokenizing is defined as focusing on a student whose identity connects with a topic of discussion and asking that student to speak on behalf of that group. Many MLs of different backgrounds report they feel singled out when their cultures or languages become the subject of a class discussion. Teachers can inadvertently create more discomfort for MLs when they are used to boost the teachers' ideas or opinions or put them on the spot.

Here are some ideas on how to mitigate tokenizing:

1. With consistency, choose a variety of students who have a range of diverse experiences and opinions to participate.
2. Engage as many students as possible in every possible circumstance.
3. Treat and tell students that they are experts in their own experience in schools, and do activities that reinforce their expertise right now. At the same time, do not push them to share if they are uncomfortable. Check ahead of time.
4. Avoid any representative activities that creates a situation where MLs are to act as officials of that identity.
5. Reach out to individual MLs ahead of time if you feel they may have something to contribute to a conversation and ask if they would like to share or not.
6. Infuse all students' voices every day through regular classroom activities, extracurricular activities, and things students already do.
7. Practice mutual accountability with students through student-led evaluations of you and your work, whether you're a teacher, program director, or student leader.
8. When you ask students to share on a specific topic, make sure there are a variety of perspectives and not just ones you agree with.
9. Provide a variety of topic options and then encourage MLs to decide which issues are important for them to share with the class.

Trauma

"In a trauma-informed school, the adults in the school community are prepared to recognize and respond to those who have been impacted by traumatic stress. Those adults include administrators, teachers, staff, parents, and law enforcement. In addition, students are provided with clear expectations and communication strategies to guide them through stressful situations. The goal is to not only provide tools to cope with extreme situations but to create an underlying culture of respect and support." NCTSN Child Trauma Toolkit for Educators www.nctsn.org/resources/child-trauma-toolkit-educators

Many MLs have experienced trauma before coming to the United States or while adjusting. A painful move from a culture and country with which they are familiar to a new one can be traumatic. Events or circumstances may include the actual or extreme threat of physical or psychological harm or the severe withholding of resources for healthy development. It's important to note that an event may be experienced as traumatic by one person and not another. The experience may be influenced by cultural beliefs and the developmental stage of the individual, among other factors. Adverse effects may occur immediately or over time. Effects may include physical, mental, emotional, cognitive, behavioral, social, and spiritual challenges.

If you come to know an ML personally, you will hear a number of traumatic events that have affected their lives.

Here's just one example from Harrison, 17 years old:

> I was born in El Salvador and came to this country two years ago. My mother left to the United States to find work when I was 5 years old. She left me and my younger brother in the care of my uncle who wasn't very nice and would mistreat us. We were very poor and my uncle would use the money my mother would send him for alcohol.
>
> I tried to attend school but I needed to provide for my brother and I. When I turned 13 I stopped going and instead began to work. In my area there were a lot of violence due to gangs and I saw many of my close friends get killed because they would not join the gang or they did something to anger the gang.
>
> At 15, I decided to escape my country because I didn't want to be a part of the gangs . I wanted to go find my mother. I made my journey through Mexico to cross the border into the U.S. I had to pay the coyotes a lot of money, but when I ran out along the way they held me with a gun in my face and called my family in the United States to force them to send more money or I would get killed.
>
> Once I was free I made my way across the border and walked through a very hot desert where Immigration found me and put me into a juvenile detention center. After they reunited me with my mother's family in New Jersey, I had a very tough time getting used to this new environment. I finally was able to see my mother, but our relationship was never the same. We have many problems and I feel

> angry that she left us so long ago. I feel a lot of anger and sadness. I love soccer so I have become a part of our soccer team which has helped me with my anger and sadness. I hope to be able to find a good job so that I can bring my younger brother.[1]

"The Core Experiences of psychological trauma are disempowerment and disconnection. Recovery, therefore, is based upon empowerment of the survivor and the creation of new connections. Recovery can take place only in the context of relationships; it cannot occur in isolation. In her renewed connections with other people, the survivor re-creates the psychological faculties that were damaged or deformed by the traumatic experience. These faculties include the basic capacities for trust, autonomy, initiative, competence, identity and intimacy," said Judith Herman, MD.

Teachers are not social workers or psychologists, even though it might seem that way at times. MLs with severe trauma should be referred to school counselors. Nevertheless, there are some practices that could be helpful within your classroom. Below are some ideas adapted from How to Help a Traumatized Child in the Classroom by Dorado and Zakrzewski (2013).

1) Awareness is a key start. When teachers recognize that a child is going into survival mode and respond in a kind, compassionate way—"What's happening here?" vs. "What's wrong with this child?"—students feel genuine care.

2) Create calm, predictable transitions in your classroom routines. This doesn't mean that you have to give up variety within the classroom, but students should know what to expect for the day. Writing your essential questions and activities on the board is helpful. Your students should know:

    a) what the transition is going to look like,

    b) what they're supposed to be doing, and

    c) what's next.

3) Praise MLs publicly and criticize privately. Nurture the students even more than you might think is necessary. Notice those moments when the student is doing really well and point it out to build their self-worth: "Wow, I noticed how Jorge helped translate that new word for Carla," or "Thank you for taking a risk and reading that passage for the class." When you need to re-direct the behavior, do so privately and in as calm a voice as possible.

4) Consider implementing a "mindful minute" before your class begins. You could play the short three-minute daily meditation from Headspace, or you could have them close their eyes or look at a spot in front of them so that no one feels like others are watching them. Tell them you will put on the timer for one to two minutes and you want them to work on breathing. They can count their breaths silently.

---

1 Trauma and Resilience: An Adolescent Provider Toolkit; Adolescent Health Working Group

Of course, the ideas I've shared are just the bare minimum when it comes to trauma-informed practices that can support MLs. I encourage you to do more research and enroll in workshops to further your background knowledge and expand your toolbox in this area. I hope that by sharing a few ideas, I've given you a starting point for creating a soft landing place for these students.

Conclusion

I'm confident that the tools in this essential guide can provide you with a starting point to help MLs connect with you, their classmates, and your class content. By implementing the 5 Cs of Classroom Set-up, Community, Context for Content, Collaboration for Content, and Choice for Assessment, you will be well on your way to enhancing your classroom not only for MLs but for everyone who gets to interact in more meaningful ways because of your practice.

Notes

1 www.qtel.wested.org

2 Dover, Alison G., and Fernando Ferran Rodríguez-Valls. Radically Inclusive Teaching with Newcomer and Emergent Plurilingual Students: Braving Up. Teachers College Press, 2022.

3 Flores, Nelson, and Jonathan Rosa. "Undoing appropriateness: Raciolinguistic ideologies and language diversity in education." Harvard educational review 85.2 (2015): 149-171.

4 Paris, Django, and H. Samy Alim, eds. Culturally sustaining pedagogies: Teaching and learning for justice in a changing world. Teachers College Press, 2017.

5 García, Ofelia, and Rosario Torres-Guevara. "11 Monoglossic Ideologies and Language Policies in the Education of US Latinas/os." Handbook of Latinos and education: Theory, research, and practice (2009): 182.

6 Cummins, Jim. "Cognitive/Academic Language Proficiency, Linguistic Interdependence, the Optimum Age Question and Some Other Matters. Working Papers on Bilingualism, No. 19." (1979).

7 Krashen, Stephen D. "The input hypothesis: Issues and implications." (1985).

8 Tarone, Elaine, and Merrill Swain. "A sociolinguistic perspective on second language use in immersion classrooms." The Modern Language Journal 79.2 (1995): 166-178.

9 Valdés, Guadalupe. "Lati Paris, Django, and H. Samy Alim, eds. Culturally sustaining pedagogies: Teaching and learning for justice in a changing world. Teachers College Press, 2017

10 Wright, Wayne E. "The political spectacle of Arizona's Proposition 203." Educational Policy 19.5 (2005): 662-700.

11 Oxford, Rebecca L., and Christina Gkonou. "Interwoven: Culture, language, and learning strategies." Studies in Second Language Learning and Teaching 8.2 (2018): 403-426.

12 Paris, Django, and H. Samy Alim, eds. Culturally sustaining pedagogies: Teaching and learning for justice in a changing world. Teachers College Press, (2017)

13 García, Ofelia, Kate Seltzer, and Daria Witt. "Disrupting linguistic inequalities in US urban classrooms: The role of translanguaging." The multilingual edge of education (2018): 41-66.

14 González, Norma, Luis C. Moll, and Cathy Amanti, eds. Funds of knowledge: Theorizing practices in households, communities, and classrooms. Routledge, 2006.

15 WIDA wida.wisc.edu

16 Barrett, Peter, Fay Davies, Yufan Zhang, and Lucinda Barrett. "The impact of classroom design on pupils' learning: Final results of a holistic, multi-level analysis." Building and Environment 89 (2015): 118-133.

17 Ferlazzo, Larry, and Katie Hull Sypnieski. The ELL Teacher's Toolbox: Hundreds of Practical Ideas to Support Your Students. John Wiley & Sons, 2018.

18 Cheryan, Sapna, et al. "Designing classrooms to maximize student achievement." Policy Insights from the Behavioral and Brain Sciences 1.1 (2014): 4-12.

19 Richards, Blake A., and Paul W. Frankland. "The persistence and transience of memory." Neuron 94.6 (2017): 1071-1084.

20 Bui, Dung C., and Mark A. McDaniel. "Enhancing learning during lecture note-taking using outlines and illustrative diagrams." Journal of Applied Research in Memory and Cognition 4.2 (2015): 129-135.

21 Barrett, Nathan, et al. "Working with what they have: Professional development as a reform strategy in rural schools." Journal of Research in Rural Education (Online) 30.10 (2015): 1.

22 Cheryan, Sapna, et al. "Designing classrooms to maximize student achievement." Policy Insights from the Behavioral and Brain Sciences 1.1 (2014): 4-12.

23 Barrett, Nathan, et al. "Working with what they have: Professional development as a reform strategy in rural schools." Journal of Research in Rural Education (Online) 30.10 (2015): 1.

24 bell hooks, Teaching to Transgress: Education as the Practice of Freedom (Oxfordshire, England: Routledge, 1994).

25 www.ed.gov

26 García, Ofelia, and Rosario Torres-Guevara. "11 Monoglossic Ideologies and Language Policies in the Education of US Latinas/os." Handbook of Latinos and education: Theory, research, and practice (2009): 182.

27 Coles-Ritchie, Marilee, and Robin Renee Smith. "Taking the risk to engage in race talk: Professional development in elementary schools." International Journal of Inclusive Education 21.2 (2017): 172-186.

28 Cajete, Gregory A. "Children, myth and storytelling: An Indigenous perspective." Global Studies of Childhood 7.2 (2017): 113-130.

29 González, Norma, Luis C. Moll, and Cathy Amanti, eds. Funds of knowledge: Theorizing practices in households, communities, and classrooms. Routledge, 2006.

30 Paul Gorski Equity Website

31 Snyder, Sydney, and Diane Staehr Fenner. Culturally responsive teaching for multilingual learners: Tools for equity. Corwin, 2021.

32 Germán, Lorena Escoto. Textured teaching: A framework for culturally sustaining practices. Heinemann, 2021.

33 Muhammad, Gholdy, et al. Unearthing joy: A guide to culturally and historically responsive curriculum and instruction. Scholastic Inc, 2023.

34 Cummins, Jim. Bilingualism and Minority-Language Children. Language and Literacy

Series. The Ontario Institute for Studies in Education, 252 Bloor Street West, Toronto, Ontario M5S 1V6, 1981.

35 Cummins, Jim. "Empowering minority students: A framework for intervention." Harvard educational review 56.1 (1986): 18-37.

36 Cummins, Jim. Rethinking the education of multilingual learners: A critical analysis of theoretical concepts. Vol. 19. Multilingual Matters, 2021.

37 Gaunt, Amy, and Alice Stott. Transform teaching and learning through talk: the oracy imperative. Rowman & Littlefield, 2018.

38 Riches, Caroline, and Fred Genesee. "Literacy: Crosslinguistic and crossmodal issues." Educating English language learners: A synthesis of research evidence (2006): 64-108.

39 Soto-Hinman, Ivannia. "Increasing Academic Oral Language Development: Using English Language Learner Shadowing in Classrooms." Multicultural Education 18.2 (2011): 21-23.

40 Mohr, Kathleen AJ, and Eric S. Mohr. "Extending English language learners' classroom interactions using the Response Protocol." The Reading Teacher 60.5 (2007): 440-450.

41 Wessels, Stephanie. "Science as a second language: Integrating science and vocabulary instruction for English language learners." (2013).

42 Rodríguez, Diane, Angela Carrasquillo, and Kyung Soon Lee. The bilingual advantage: Promoting academic development, biliteracy, and native language in the classroom. Teachers College Press, 2014.

43 californiascienceproject.ucr.edu

44 Gibbons, Pauline. Scaffolding language, scaffolding learning. Portsmouth, NH: Heinemann, 2002.

45 Walqui, Aída, and Leo Van Lier. Scaffolding the academic success of adolescent English language learners: A pedagogy of promise. WestEd. 2010.

46 García, Ofelia, and Tatyana Kleyn, eds. Translanguaging with multilingual students: Learning from classroom moments. Routledge, 2016.

47 Westernoff, Fern, Stephaney Jones-Vo, and Paula Markus. Powerful practices for supporting English learners: Elevating diverse assets and identities. Corwin, 2021.

48 Calderón, Margarita Espino, and Liliana Minaya-Rowe. Preventing long-term ELs: Transforming schools to meet core standards. Corwin Press, 2010.

49 Coles-Ritchie, Marilee. Inciting change in secondary English language programs: The case of Cherry High School. Springer, 2009.

50 Haynes, Judie, and Debbie Zacarian. Teaching English language learners across the content areas. ASCD, 2010.

51 Gottlieb, Margo. Assessing English language learners: Bridges to educational equity: Connecting academic language proficiency to student achievement. Corwin Press, 2016.

52 Table adapted from californiascienceproject.ucr.edu

53 ahwg.org/download/trauma-and-resilience-2013

Glossary of Language Terms

Academic English: The English language ability required for academic achievement in context-reduced situations, such as classroom lectures and textbook reading assignments. This is sometimes referred to as Cognitive/Academic Language Proficiency (CALP).

Affective filter: a metaphor that describes a learner's feelings of anxiety or attitudes that affect their ability to learn an additional language. Feelings such as lack of motivation, self-confidence, and anxiety can act as filters that hinder and obstruct language learning. This term is associated with linguist Stephen Krashen's Monitor Model of language learning.

Authentic assessment: a process using multiple forms of evaluation that reflect student learning, achievement, motivation, and attitudes on classroom activities. Examples include performance assessment, portfolios, and student self-assessment.

Automaticity: a term that refers to any skilled and complex behavior that can be performed easily with little attention, effort, or conscious awareness. These skills become automatic after extended periods of usage. With practice and ongoing instruction, students become automatic at word recognition by retrieving words from memory and are able to focus attention on constructing meaning from the text, rather than decoding.

Basic interpersonal communication skills (BICS): often referred to as "social language." It is the basic language ability required for face-to-face communication where linguistic interactions are embedded in a situational context. BICS is part of a theory of language proficiency developed by Jim Cummins. BICS, which is highly contextualized and often accompanied by gestures, is cognitively undemanding and relies on context to aid understanding.

Bilingual education: a program in which two languages are used to provide content-matter instruction. Bilingual education programs vary in their length of time and in the amount each language is used.

Bilingualism: the ability to use two languages. Defining bilingualism can be problematic, since proficiency across the four language dimensions (listening, speaking, reading, and writing) and differences in proficiency between the two languages can be difficult to measure.

Biliteracy: the ability to effectively communicate or understand a language by writing or reading, including being aware of grammatical systems, vocabularies, and written symbols of two different languages.

Castañeda v. Pickard: a landmark case for Multilingual Learners (MLs). On June 23, 1981, the Fifth Circuit Court issued a decision that is the seminal post-Lau decision concerning education of language-minority students. The case established a three-part test to evaluate the adequacy of a district's program for MLs: (1) Is the program based on an educational theory recognized as sound by some experts in the field or is considered by experts as a legitimate experimental strategy? (2) Are the programs and practices, including resources and personnel, reasonably calculated to implement this theory effectively? and (3) Does the school district evaluate its programs and make adjustments where needed to ensure language barriers are actually being overcome? 648 F.2d 989 (5th Cir., 1981)

Center for Applied Linguistics (CAL): a private, non-profit organization consisting of a group of scholars and educators who use the findings of linguistics to identify and address language-related problems. CAL carries out a wide range of activities including research, teacher education, analysis and dissemination of information, design and development of instructional materials, technical assistance, conference planning, program evaluation, and policy analysis. Visit the CAL website for more information.

Cognates: words in different languages related to the same root, such as education (English) and educación (Spanish).

Cognitive/academic language proficiency (CALP): the language ability required for academic achievement in schooling in a context-reduced environment. Examples of context-reduced environments include classroom lectures and textbook reading assignments, where there are few environmental cues (facial expressions, gestures, visuals) that help students understand the content. CALP is part of a theory of language developed by Jim Cummins.

Content-based English: This approach makes use of instructional materials, learning tasks, and classroom techniques from academic content areas as the vehicle for developing language, content, and cognitive and study skills. English is used as the medium of instruction, but translanguaging methods can also be employed.

Context clues: sources of information in text that readers may use to predict the identities and meanings of unknown words. Context clues may be drawn from the immediate sentence containing the word, text already read, pictures accompanying the text, or definitions, restatements, examples, or descriptions in the text.

Context-embedded language: communication that occurs in a context of shared understanding, where there are cues or signals that help create meaning (e.g., visuals, gestures, facial expressions, locations).

Context-reduced language: communication where there are few clues about the meaning of the communication apart from the words themselves. The language is likely to be abstract and academic, such as classroom lectures or books without pictures.

Dialogue journals: journals that involve more than one person writing ideas in the same notebook or journal. For example, a student writes an idea on a topic and then asks a question. The respondent, usually the teacher, answers the questions and writes a question back again.

Differentiated instruction: teaching that includes planning out and executing various approaches to content, process, and product to meet the needs of students with a variety of differences in readiness, interests, and learning needs.

Digital literacy: the ability to effectively navigate, evaluate, and generate information using digital technology (e.g., computers, software, digital devices, the internet).

Dual-language program: a bilingual education program designed to support students' development with all four language skills (listening, speaking, reading, and writing) in two languages. Instruction is taught through both languages usually for about the same amount of time.

English as a second language (ESL): refers to a student acquiring English as an additional language. The term is no longer used widely, as the assumption that English is a student's second language is not always accurate. ESL instruction is usually in English, with little use of students' other languages.

English language development (ELD): instruction designed specifically for multilingual learners to develop their listening, speaking, reading, and writing skills in English. This type of instruction is also known by many different terms (depending on the district), such as:

- English as a second language (ESL)
- English for speakers of other languages (ESOL)
- English as a new language (ENL)
- English language learner (ELL) instruction
- English learner (EL) instruction

English language proficiency (ELP): the focus of academic language's four domains of language (listening, reading, speaking, writing) for all subject areas. Every state is required to have its own set of ELP standards that describe what a student should be able to do in English in each domain and at each level of English proficiency.

Equal Education Opportunities Act of 1974: This civil rights statute prohibits states from denying equal educational opportunity to an individual on account of race, color, sex, or national origin. The statute specifically prohibits states from denying equal educational opportunity by an educational agency's failure to take appropriate action to overcome language barriers that impede equal participation by its students in its instructional programs. 20 U.S.C. §1203(f)

Informed parental consent: the written permission of a parent or guardian to enroll their child in an English learning or English Language Development program, or the refusal to allow their child to enroll in such a program, after the parent is provided effective notice of the educational options and the district's educational recommendation.

Maintenance bilingual education (MBE), also referred to as "late-exit bilingual education": a program that uses two languages, the student's primary language and English, as a means of instruction. The instruction builds upon the student's primary-language skills and develops and expands the English language skills of each student to enable them to achieve proficiency in both languages while providing access to the content areas.

Multilingual learner (ML): students who are in the process of learning English and other languages. Because the U.S. system is primarily in English, the language emphasis is usually placed on English. While many MLs are immigrants or refugees, the majority are born in the United States.

Other names for this student population:

- English learners (ELs)
- Dual-language learners
- Bilingual students
- Diverse-language learners

Name for programs of English instruction:

- English as a second language (ESL)
- English for speakers of other languages (ESOL)
- English language development (ELD)
- English as a new language (ENL)
- English language learner (ELL) instruction
- English learner (EL) instruction
- Limited English Proficient (LEP)
  *While the federal government used this term for a long time, it has generally been phased out in favor of more asset-based focus terminology.

Exit criteria: guidelines for ending special services for MLs and placing them in mainstream, English-only classes as fluent or close to fluent English speakers. To exit, students usually need to pass an English language proficiency test, have passing grades, meet basic standardized test scores, and/or get a teacher's recommendations. In some cases, this redesignation of students may be based on the amount of time they have been in special programs.

First language: a student's first language, sometimes referred to as "L1." It's important to note that a student's first language may not be their primary or dominant language.

Formal assessment: information gathered on a student using standardized, published tests or instruments in conjunction with specific administration and interpretation procedures, and used to make general instructional decisions.

Formative assessments: Frequent evaluations of students that help a teacher make adjustments in instruction to help students reach target achievement goals. These are almost always designed by students and assessed in the classroom setting.

Graphic organizers: text, diagram, or other pictorial devices that summarize and/or illustrate interrelationships among concepts in a text. Graphic organizers are often known as maps, webs, graphs, charts, frames, or clusters.

Home language: the language most often spoken at home. Sometimes this term is interchanged with dominant, first, mother tongue, native, or primary, but they all have distinctions. A student's home language might not be their first or primary language.

Individualized Education Program (IEP): a plan outlining special education and related services specifically designed to meet the unique educational needs of a student who is differently abled.

Language majority: refers to the dominant or most widely used language of a country. In the United States, it is English. Note that the United States does not have an official language at the federal level.

Language minority: refers to a language other than the dominant, societal, or most commonly spoken language.

Language proficiency: a measurement of how a person effectively communicates, understands thoughts or ideas, knows the grammatical system and its vocabulary, and/or uses its sounds or written symbols. Language proficiency includes the four domains of listening, reading, speaking, and writing.

Lau vs. Nichols: a 1974 lawsuit filed by Chinese parents in San Francisco. This suit led to a landmark Supreme Court ruling that "identical education" does not constitute "equal education" under the Civil Rights Act. School districts must take "affirmative steps" to overcome educational barriers faced by students from language groups other than English. Lau remedies are policy guidelines for the education of Multilingual Learners and require that school districts comply with the civil rights requirements of Title VI.

Limited English proficient (LEP): the term used by the federal government, most states, and local school districts to identify those students who have insufficient English to succeed in English-only classrooms. Most experts consider this term outdated because it is based on deficits and does not accurately describe multilingual learners. Terms such as "English language learner" (ELL) or "English learner" (EL) are most commonly used in place of LEP.

Local Education Agency (LEA): a public board of education or other public authority within a state that maintains administrative control of public elementary or secondary schools in a city, county, township, school district, or other political subdivision of a state.

Long-term English-language learner (LTELL): a student who has been enrolled in U.S. schools for more than six years but has not reached grade-level proficiency in English, determined by standardized assessments.

Mainstream: refers to a typical classroom that almost all students attend. The goal of most school programs is to exit MLs into mainstream classes as quickly as possible. Some MLs are placed in mainstream classes when they are at the beginning stages of proficiency.

Mother tongue: refers to the language a child first learned to speak.

Native language: the first language a child acquires or identifies with as a member of a collective group. This term variably means (a) the language learned from the care givers, (b) the first language learned, (c) the native language of an area or country, (d) the stronger (or primary) language at any time of life, (e) the language used most often by a person. This is sometimes interchanged with mother tongue, primary language, home language, or dominant language.

Natural Approach: a methodology for learning an additional language by focusing on communicative skills, both oral and written. Stephen Krashen promoted this theory of language acquisition in opposition to the more passive repetitive way of teaching language that was used in the '60s. It suggests that speech emerges in four stages: (1) preproduction (listening and gestures), (2) early production (short phrases), (3) speech emergence (long phrases and sentences), and (4) intermediate fluency (conversation).

Newcomer program: focuses on the needs of recent immigrant students, most commonly at the secondary level who are at the earliest stages of development in English in a separate, relatively self-contained building or classroom. Newcomer programs provide a sheltered environment with other MLs so they can work on English language skills, understand U.S. school culture, and learn vocabulary of core academics. Some newcomer programs also include primary-language development and an orientation to the student's new community. Typically, students attend these programs before they enter more traditional interventions (e.g., English language development programs or mainstream classrooms with supplemental ML instruction).

Office of Civil Rights (OCR): a branch of the U.S. Department of Education that investigates allegations of civil rights violations in schools. It also initiates investigations of compliance with federal civil rights laws in schools that serve special student populations, including MLs. Several policies are in place to measure compliance with the Lau v. Nichols decision. OCR is also responsible for enforcing Title VI of the Civil Rights Act of 1964. For more information, see the OCR resources about ELLs and OCR Disability Discrimination: Overview of the Laws.

Phonemic awareness: the ability to notice, think about, and work with the individual sounds in spoken words. An example of how beginning readers show they have phonemic awareness is when they can combine or blend the separate sounds of a word.

Phonics: matching the sounds of spoken languages with individual letters or groups of letters. It emphasizes the predictable relationship between phonemes (the sounds in spoken language) and graphemes (the letters that represent those sounds in written language) and demonstrates how this information can be used to read or decode words.

Phonological awareness: the awareness of and ability to work with sounds in spoken language, which sets the stage for decoding, blending, and, ultimately, word reading. Phonological awareness begins developing before the beginning of formal schooling and continues through third grade and beyond.

Portfolio assessment: a systematic collection of student work that is analyzed to show progress over time with regard to instructional objectives or standards. Student portfolios may include responses to readings, samples of writing, drawings, or other work.

Primary language: the language with which multilingual speaker has greatest proficiency and/or uses most often. Used interchangeably with dominant language.

Productive language: the two language skills that are produced by the language learners: speaking and writing.

Proficiency in language: measuring a student's performance based on criterion established in the core or standards as measured by a teacher or a standardized assessment, often paired with independent(ly) to suggest a successful student performance done without scaffolding. In the reading standards, the act of reading a text with comprehension. See also independent(ly) scaffolding.

Pull-out English for Speakers of Other Languages: a program in which MLs are "pulled out" of regular, mainstream classrooms for special instruction in English. In secondary schools, students are not pulled out of classes but they most likely will attend an English Language Development class within their school day. They are usually labeled as Level 1–4 in conjunction with their WIDA score or other measurement.

Receptive language: the two language skills that are received by the language learners: listening and reading.

Scaffolding: guidance or assistance a teacher, another adult, or a more capable peer provides a student, enabling them to perform a task they otherwise would not be able to do alone, with the goal of fostering the student's capacity to perform the task on their own later on.

Semantic map: a strategy for graphically representing concepts. As a strategy, semantic maps involve expanding a student's vocabulary by encouraging new links to familiar concepts. Instructionally, semantic maps can be used for all kinds of activities for charting what is known about a concept, theme, or individual word. They are also helpful for organizing ideas for projects or papers.

Sheltered English instruction: an instructional approach that makes academic instruction in English understandable to MLs. In the sheltered classroom, teachers use as much context as possible, such as physical activities, visual aids, and the environment, to make content accessible in mathematics, science, social studies, and other subjects.

Standard English: considered the most widely accepted form of English, adhering to fixed academic norms of spelling, grammar, and usage in written and spoken contexts, and neutralizing nonstandard dialectal variation. It is sometimes referred to as "school English." It does not have any more inherent worth than any other form of English.

Submersion program: a plan that places MLs in a regular English-only program with little or no support services, on the theory that they will pick up English naturally. Leaving students to "sink or swim," it is the least effective of all programs for MLs.

Summative assessment: evaluations generally carried out at the end of a course or project. In an educational setting, summative assessments are typically used to assign students a course grade.

Teachers of English to Speakers of Other Languages (TESOL) Organization: a professional association of teachers, administrators, researchers, and others concerned with promoting and strengthening instruction and research in the teaching of English to speakers of other languages.

Title VI of the Civil Rights Act of 1964: Title VI prohibits discrimination on the grounds of race, color, or national origin against recipients of federal financial assistance. The Title VI regulatory requirements have been interpreted to prohibit denial of equal access to education because of a language-minority student's limited proficiency in English.

Title VII of the Elementary and Secondary Education Act: The Bilingual Education Act, Title VII of the Elementary and Secondary Education Act (ESEA), recognizes the unique educational disadvantages faced by non-English speaking students. Enacted in 1968, the Bilingual Education Act established a federal policy to assist educational agencies to serve students with limited English proficiency by authorizing funding to support those efforts. In addition to providing funds to support services to "limited-English-proficient students," Title VII also supports professional development and research activities. Reauthorized in 1994 as part of the Improving America's Schools Act, Title VII was restructured to provide for an increased state role and give priority to applicants seeking to develop bilingual proficiency. The Improving America's Schools

Act also modified eligibility requirements for services under Title I so that limited-English-proficient students are eligible for services under that program on the same basis as other students.

Total physical response (TPR): a language-learning approach based on the relationship between language and its physical representation or execution. TPR emphasizes the use of physical activity for increasing meaningful learning opportunities and language retention. A TPR lesson involves a detailed series of consecutive actions accompanied by a teacher's series of commands or instructions. Students respond by listening and performing the appropriate actions.

Transitional bilingual education (TBE): an educational program in which two languages are used to provide content-matter instruction. Over time, the use of the primary language is decreased and the use of English is increased until only English is used.

Universal design for learning (UDL): provides a framework for creating flexible goals, methods, materials, and assessments that accommodate learner differences that start with questions rather than set objectives.

About the Author

Marilee Coles-Ritchie is an education expert specializing in teaching Multilingual Learners with equity. She has experience working in the field of language acquisition and multicultural education for 35+ years. She has taught Multilingual Learners in many diverse settings, including a public high school in Douglas, Arizona, a bilingual secondary school in Quito, Ecuador, and an elementary school in the Navajo Nation. She has a Master of Teaching degree in TESOL (Teaching English to Speakers of Other Languages) and a PhD in Cultural and Social Foundations of Education, emphasizing language education. She teaches educational foundations, qualitative research methods, and TESOL endorsement courses as a Full Professor at Westminster University in Salt Lake City, Utah.

Learn more and subscribe to her newsletter: marileecolesritchie.com

Made in the USA
Coppell, TX
07 July 2025

51590818R00063